The MYTH of the LITIGIOUS SOCIETY

THE CHICAGO SERIES

IN LAW AND SOCIETY

Edited by John M. Conley

and Lynn Mather

David M. Engel

The MYTH
of the
LITIGIOUS
SOCIETY

Why We Don't Sue

THE
UNIVERSITY
OF
CHICAGO
PRESS
Chicago and London

The University of Chicago Press, Chicago 60637

The University of Chicago Press, Ltd., London

© 2016 by The University of Chicago

Published 2016.

Printed in the United States of America

25 24 23 22 21 20 19 18 17 16   1 2 3 4 5

ISBN-13: 978-0-226-30504-2 (cloth)

ISBN-13: 978-0-226-30518-9 (e-book)

DOI: 10.7208/chicago/9780226305189.001.0001

Library of Congress Cataloging-in-Publication Data

Names: Engel, David M., author.

Title: The myth of the litigious society : why we don't sue / David M. Engel.

Other titles: Chicago series in law and society.

Description: Chicago : The University of Chicago Press, 2016. | Series: Chicago series in law and society

Identifiers: LCCN 2016000009 | ISBN 9780226305042 (cloth : alk. paper) | ISBN 9780226305189 (e-book)

Subjects: LCSH: Personal injuries—Social aspects—United States. | Personal injuries—United States—Psychological aspects. | Accident victims—United States—Psychology. | Torts—Social aspects—United States.

Classification: LCC KF1251 .E54 2016 | DDC 346.7303—dc23 LC record available at http://lccn.loc.gov/2016000009

♾ This paper meets the requirements of ANSI/NISO Z39.48–1992 (Permanence of Paper).

TO JARUWAN, *who made everything possible*

CONTENTS

ONE

THE CASE OF THE
MISSING PLAINTIFF

‖‖‖

If most of us were asked why physically injured Americans rarely sue, we would probably think the question itself makes no sense. Everyone knows that we live in a highly litigious society, probably the most litigious on earth. We sue one another at the slightest provocation and view injuries as a chance to strike it rich. Politicians decry our insatiable appetite for the law, and legislatures have embraced "tort reform" in a vain attempt to slow the lawsuit juggernaut. Shouldn't we ask why Americans sue so much rather than so little?

In this instance, however, the thing that everyone knows for sure just ain't so.[1] Researchers have repeatedly confirmed a surprising fact about injured Americans—the vast majority do not sue and do not even consult lawyers. Instead, even when they've been harmed by someone else's wrongful act and suffered serious loss, most injury victims make no attempt to hold the injurer responsible—in court or anywhere else. The reluctance of victims to confront their injurers is an empirical fact, though it directly contradicts what most Americans believe to be true of themselves and their fellow citizens. In the next chapter, we

1

will explore more closely just how seldom it is that people with injuries assert a claim or invoke the law.

If it's true that most Americans don't insist on their rights, even when they suffer physical injuries after being wronged by another, then the premise of our question is not as ridiculous as it might seem. Why do claims and lawsuits occur so infrequently? What really needs to be explained is not our passion for litigation but the dog that doesn't bark. In the famous Sherlock Holmes story "Silver Blaze," Holmes shrewdly recognizes that the fact demanding explanation is the silence—the *inactivity* of a dog living at the site of an apparent murder. Holmes insists on the importance of this nonevent in a dialogue with Colonel Ross, a "well-known sportsman," who employed the murder victim:

> "Is there any point to which you would wish to draw my attention?"
>
> "To the curious incident of the dog in the night-time."
>
> "The dog did nothing in the night-time."
>
> "That was the curious incident," remarked Sherlock Holmes.[2]

That is how Sir Arthur Conan Doyle renders the dialogue between Holmes and Ross. Suppose, however, that the two men had continued their discussion along the following lines:

> "Quite right," responded Colonel Ross, "We need to do something about that dog's infernal barking in the night-time."
>
> "No, no, you misunderstand me, Colonel. The dog didn't bark at all. *That's* the fact that demands explanation."
>
> "We must pass a new ordinance cracking down on dog owners who allow their animals to make so much noise and disrupt the entire neighborhood. I will approach the town

council tomorrow and recommend that we once and for all get this dog barking problem under control."

"Colonel Ross, please focus more carefully on the facts we have uncovered. What we need to explain is not why the dog barked but why he was silent. Let's pay attention to the actual evidence here!"

"Holmes, this epidemic of dog-barking is completely out of control. It is destroying the social fabric and moral character of the British people. Dog owners in our country have to demonstrate a greater sense of responsibility, and we should bring the full weight of the law to bear on this problem."

Speechless and exasperated, Holmes gnashes his teeth, then mutters a possibly obscene deprecation under his breath.

ASKING WHY THE DOG DOESN'T BARK

Much depends on determining why the dog in the story didn't bark—its silence provides the key that unlocks the mystery and identifies the murderer. So it is understandable that Holmes would experience utter frustration if Colonel Ross ignored the problem that presented itself—the dog's inactivity—and went on instead about solutions to a problem for which there was no credible evidence at all.

Yet that is precisely what has happened in discussions about injuries and lawsuits in America. The inactivity of injury victims, reconfirmed in study after study, has been ignored as a problem that demands explanation. Instead, specious claims of a litigation explosion have been made so often that they have rooted themselves in the national psyche and now seem too obvious to question. Researchers have decisively refuted the myth of litigiousness, but legislatures across the country have nevertheless adopted "tort reform" measures aimed at curbing the imagined proliferation of injury litigation. Some defenders of the tort law system have challenged these efforts, but almost no one has attempted to ask or answer the more basic and arguably the most important question, *why doesn't the dog bark?*

This question has fascinated me for many years. I am a law professor who teaches torts, which is the branch of our civil justice system that requires people, corporations, and sometimes governments to pay damages when they have violated a legal duty of care and caused harm. I find the phenomenon of the injury victim who doesn't claim deeply puzzling. It contradicts everything we have read or heard in the media about our lawsuit-prone society. It even violates the assumptions that tort experts themselves make about the behavior of injury victims. Yet I could find almost no research aimed at explaining why the dog doesn't bark in injury cases. I eventually concluded that the question was important enough to justify an all-out search for clues that might solve the mystery, including insights from disciplines quite remote from my own, such as rehabilitation science, nursing, anesthesiology, and neuroscience. This book presents the results of my investigation.

INJURIES AS A SOCIAL PROBLEM

Each year, enormous numbers of injuries befall Americans and impair their lives, sometimes with devastating consequences. The National Safety Council surveyed accidents in the year 2012 and found that nearly one in every eight Americans suffered physical injuries that were serious enough to require medical treatment. That's over 38 million Americans seriously injured in a single year—and another 127,200 were killed. More than half of these injuries occurred in the home, another 12.8 percent at work, and 10.2 percent were associated with motor vehicles.[3] Each year, our country experiences a huge number of injuries, a portion of which no doubt occurs because of a wrong committed by someone else. Yet, large as these numbers are, they are greatly understated. The true injury problem is even worse. The NSC confined its survey to physical harms resulting from "accidents." It didn't include *illnesses* or degenerative conditions caused by wrongful conduct—such as toxic exposures or the sale of negligently designed pharmaceuticals. It did not attempt to count the hundreds of thousands of injuries and fatalities caused by errors in medical treatment or care. And it omitted nonphysical injuries that sometimes lead to physical setbacks, such as the infliction of emotional distress, acts of discrimination, slurs, and bullying. From a legal perspective, all of these harms are also considered injuries. If they were added to the figures in the NSC survey, the number of Americans injured each year would be shockingly large.

So yes, America does have an injury problem. But what is noteworthy about our response is not that too many unworthy claimants bring lawsuits at the drop of a hat. Rather, it is that more than nine out of ten injury victims assert no claim at all against their injurer—even in cases where it is likely that a legal duty was breached and a claim would succeed. In this book, I shall argue that the campaign to reduce damage awards and curtail tort actions is misguided and unfair. It makes no sense to respond to the millions of injuries Americans suffer each year by reducing their access to justice. So-called tort reform has made a serious problem of injuries in our society even worse. Moreover, tort reform has failed to deliver on its promises of reduced insurance premiums and cheaper products and services.

Is the answer, then, to unleash the power of tort law and encourage vastly greater numbers of lawsuits? As one who teaches tort law, do I favor using it whenever possible? No, definitely not. The purpose of this book is *not* to argue that many more injury victims should lodge claims. The book's subtitle is "Why

We Don't Sue" and not "Let's All Litigate." Whether American society would be better off with a much higher number of lawsuits is debatable. Would we really want to live in a world where lawsuits were as common as candy? To answer that question would require another, very different book.

In my view, the tort reformers have got it wrong, with their unfounded tales of trigger-happy plaintiffs. Their highly successful public relations campaign exemplifies victim blaming at its worst. But the sworn opponents of tort reform, personal injury lawyers and others, have also misjudged the situation. They have failed to recognize that, even if tort reform could be dismantled overnight, the vast majority of injury victims would still avoid lawyers and would make no claims of any kind against their injurers. Tort reform has cut victims off from the possibility of full and fair compensation. But even if the shackles of tort reform were removed, few of them would bring a legal claim—*for reasons this book will explain.*

Although the capacity of tort law is much more limited than its defenders acknowledge, it does have an incremental social role to play, and we should not lose sight of its function because of the fog of "truthiness" generated by the tort reformers. The small minority of injury victims willing to sue does make a contribution to the public good. They are the canaries in the mineshaft, alerting society as a whole that dangerous situations exist and that negligent or reckless actors need to be called to account. High profile tort cases can trigger congressional action or encourage government agencies to issue new regulations. Personal injury lawsuits, as rare as they are, can "scare injurers straight" and deter further misconduct. And the occasional courtroom success can provide a satisfying symbolic statement about social values, about reestablishing the moral equilibrium. Tort law alone can do little to resolve our country's injury problem, no matter what the personal injury lawyers might have us believe, but it can play a necessary role in tandem with government regulation, media exposure, and market pressures.

SETTING THE SCENE

At the very outset of my effort to emulate Sherlock Holmes, then, I had to confront a peculiar contradiction within a familiar public debate. Here is the contradiction: On the one side, proponents of tort reform strenuously advocate a set of solutions for a problem that does not, objectively speaking, exist—the problem of the hyper-litigious American. On the other side, defenders of personal injury litigation assume that tort law offers a solution to the national injury problem even though the overwhelming majority of injury victims never enter a lawyer's office or make any sort of legal claim against their injurers. A crucial question cries out for explanation yet everyone seems to ignore it—what can possibly explain the reluctance of most injury victims to assert claims and invoke their rights, even when there is strong evidence that the law is on their side? Because policy opponents pay so little attention to this question, the arguments on both sides of the debate badly miss the mark.

It may be helpful at this point to provide a little background. What is tort law, and where is it meant to fit in our society's overall response to the injury problem? Where did modern tort law come from, and how did it give rise to the tort reform movement?

Injuries are a universal fact of human existence, and each society develops its own set of responses. Dostoevsky is said to have remarked, "The degree of civilization in a society can be judged by entering its prisons."[4] The same could be said of injuries—a society can be judged by how it cares for injury victims, how it sanctions injurers, how it classifies injuries, and how it reduces the risk of injury for the population as a whole.

Serious injuries can destroy lives, not only those of the direct victims but also those of their families and friends. Injuries create immediate, out-of-pocket costs, including medical bills and lost wages, and they also have long-term effects such as unemployment, dependency, and poverty. In short, injuries have serious repercussions, not just for injury victims but for society as a whole.

So what is it that American society does about injuries? We address the needs of *injury victims* by leaving many of them to fend for themselves, pay injury costs out of their own pockets, arrange their own care, and attempt to manage their own recovery. Beyond self-help, some injury victims have their needs met through their health and accident insurance, through payments by the injurer's liability insurance, through workers' compensation, and through government benefit programs such as Medicaid, Medicare, and Social Security Disability Insurance. Tort law is another mechanism by which injury victims can satisfy their post-injury needs. It operates through legal claims brought directly against the persons or companies that caused the harm.

Similarly, we address the *injurer's* behavior and responsibilities in many—perhaps most—instances through a laissez-faire approach, trusting social sanctions or market forces to pressure the injurer into offering compensation or reducing risky behavior. More interventionist approaches include the use of criminal law sanctions (fines or imprisonment for injuring another person), government regulation, and mandatory liability insurance. And, as we shall see, tort law may also play a role in sanctioning injurer misconduct and deterring others from engaging in unacceptable behavior.

The balm tort law prescribes for injuries is money, which it distributes to injury victims in two different forms. *Compensatory damages* require defendants to pay an amount that makes up for the loss they have inflicted on the plaintiff. The loss may be pecuniary (medical expenses, lost income, and other present or future out-of-pocket costs) or nonpecuniary (pain and suffering). *Punitive damages*, on the other hand, are reserved for cases involving particularly egregious behavior, what the law calls "willful or wanton" misconduct. Courts make the defendants pay punitive damages in order to punish them and deter future misdeeds. From reading the newspapers or watching TV, you might think that punitive damages are awarded in most tort cases, but in fact they are extremely rare. A recent Department of Justice study found that plaintiffs received punitive damage awards in only 3 percent of all tort cases brought in state courts, which is where most injury litigation takes place.[5]

Tort law is not some newfangled gimmick dreamed up yesterday by clever trial lawyers. It has ancient roots in Anglo-American history. But American tort law did not take its present form until the advent of the Industrial Revolution in the mid-nineteenth century. As industrial injuries skyrocketed, American judges engaged in what we nowadays might call the most sweeping "tort reform" in our history. Because of their concern that the companies spearheading our industrial development could be crippled by lawsuits, judges simply changed the rules of the game. They made it much harder for injury victims to sue by abandoning an older standard of strict liability ("if you broke it, you pay for it"), which they replaced with a new standard of negligence (no liability unless the injury victim can prove that someone committed a specific unreasonable act). Other new rules and standards protected potential defendants even further and made it extremely difficult for injury victims to recover damages. American tort law in the late nineteenth and early twentieth centuries came to be dominated by a "caveat emptor" philosophy that "swept beyond commercial dealings to the marketplace of personal injury as well: let the victim, as well as the buyer, beware."[6]

Of course there were some exceptions, and the pendulum occasionally swung in the other direction. As twentieth-century tort law evolved, it became friendlier in some ways to plaintiffs' interests. In fact, by the middle of the twentieth century, some judges in injury cases began to ask not who was at fault but who was best able to reduce the number and cost of injuries, insure against them, or redistribute costs in order to spread the burden among all those connected to an enterprise. In other words, they came to see tort law as an instrument to implement broader policies aimed at the public good and not just as a mechanism to compensate individual victims. In cases involving dangerous or defective products, some judges abandoned the negligence requirement entirely and forced injurers—who were often large corporations—to internalize the costs of injuries even when there was no proof they were at fault.

This progressive trend in mid-century tort law was a red flag for American corporations, insurance companies, hospitals, doctors, and others, who feared an expansion of their liability for injuries. By the late twentieth and early twenty-first centuries, conservative political forces launched a powerful and highly visible counterattack. They argued that concern about the rights of the injured plaintiff should be balanced or outweighed by concern for the financial well-being of American enterprises. Many judges agreed. Injury claims came to be viewed with great suspicion. Courts increasingly reaffirmed the fault principle and reversed the trend toward no-fault or strict liability approaches. The use of tort law to achieve broader public policy objectives was questioned. Innovative judicial decisions offering expanded opportunities for plaintiffs were balanced or reversed by a more cautious approach on the part of many judges.

Around this time, the term "tort reform" became a rallying cry for the critics who sought to limit injury lawsuits. Starting in the 1970s, modern tort reform scored its earliest victories by promoting medical malpractice legislation in a number of states. For example, in 1975 California enacted the Medical Injury Compensation Reform Act (MICRA),[7] which capped pain and suffering damage awards at $250,000. A RAND study determined that MICRA had the effect of reducing jury awards in medical error cases by 30 percent. Female plaintiffs and those injured the most seriously were affected more drastically than others.[8] Similar effects have been found in other states that imposed limitations on medical malpractice claims.

In the 1980s, tort reformers took on what they characterized as an "explosion" of tort litigation, asserting a direct link between injury lawsuits and skyrocketing insurance rates, although there is compelling evidence that such a link simply doesn't exist.[9] As they broadened their focus to include all types of injuries, not just those resulting from medical errors, modern tort reform took off. Responses to the alleged crisis varied across the country. Many states enacted aggressive measures spanning the entire field of tort law, including caps on pain and suffering awards and punitive damages, modification of liability rules within groups of negligent defendants, restrictions on lawyers' contingency fees, and limitations on class action suits. In addition to medical malpractice law, products liability also became a favorite target at both the state and federal levels.[10] Many judges joined the spirit of the tort reform movement, and their decisions in tort cases rolled back proplaintiff developments of the 1960s and early 1970s, including strict liability standards for dangerous and defective products.[11]

Tort reform found avid backers among conservative political candidates. Support came from think tanks such as the Manhattan Institute for Policy Research and organizations such as

the American Tort Reform Association (ATRA) and local organizations calling themselves Citizens against Lawsuit Abuse
(CALA). Ample funding was provided by tobacco companies,
other large corporations, and insurance companies.[12] Newt
Gingrich featured tort reform as one of the ten promises in
the "Contract with America" in 1994,[13] and George W. Bush adopted it in his successful gubernatorial and presidential campaigns. Tort reform's message about injuries and injury claimants began to pervade the media and the popular culture.[14]

The cultural impact of tort reform was no accident. Proponents aimed not merely to change the law, as in previous
historical cycles, but to change the way the American public
thought about injuries and civil justice.[15] Reformers conducted
a highly visible anti-tort law PR campaign in both the print
media and on TV. Their culture shift strategy has been largely
successful. Americans today hold predominantly negative
views of tort law and of the plaintiffs and lawyers associated
with tort claims. Trial lawyers find they must overcome skeptical and even hostile attitudes of prospective jurors if they are
to persuade them to consider the merits of an injury claim
objectively.[16]

AMERICANS' AMBIVALENT VIEWS OF TORT LAW

What is it about tort law that generates so much debate, controversy, and criticism, much of it misinformed if not
meretricious? The truth is Americans have always entertained
deeply conflicting views of injury claims and claimants. That's
mostly because of what tort law does in response to injuries.
Put simply, tort law converts human pain and suffering into
money. The monetization of injury is why some injury victims
value it so highly but also why it is so easy to vilify. Vilification
makes a difference. The more I investigated the case of the
missing plaintiff, the more convinced I became that our cul-

tural ambivalence toward the very idea of an injury claim for money damages has a great deal to do with the reluctance of injury victims to come forward.

Americans see tort claims through two very different lenses. On the one hand, there is the Tort Plaintiff as Champion of the People. Daring to take on the big corporations, people who bring claims expose wrongdoing and make the world safer for their fellow citizens. Think of Julia Roberts in *Erin Brockovich*. On the other hand, there is the Tort Plaintiff as Social Parasite. Americans admire those who are strong and self-sufficient in the face of adversity, and we despise people who whine, complain, and finagle for the easy buck. The iconic Hollywood heroes don't need the help of the courts or big government when things go wrong; they can take care of themselves. The Whiplash Charlies and their unscrupulous lawyers seem almost unpatriotic in their dependence on the law, their money-grubbing tricks, and their exploitation of the credulity of judges and juries. Think of *The Fortune Cookie*, in which Walter Matthau as lawyer "Whiplash Willie" Gingrich encourages Jack Lemmon to fake partial paralysis after a Cleveland Browns football player runs over him at a game. Think of Saul Goodman in *Breaking Bad*, who keeps a box of neck braces in his office to help his clients exaggerate (or fabricate) their injuries.

These two Hollywood views of tort plaintiffs—as champions of the people and as social parasites—reveal an even deeper ambivalence about culturally acceptable responses for Americans who suffer injury at the hands of a fellow citizen. Sometimes injuries come into focus quite clearly as the violation of rights. We have a right to expect others to behave responsibly and not to put us at risk unnecessarily. When a person or organization violates our rights, we should insist that the law step in and hold them accountable. At other times, however, injuries evoke an ethic of individual responsibility. Americans should take care of themselves rather than depending on others. They should guard against injuries as best they can but accept them stoically when they occur and not blame someone else. When misfortune strikes, we should suck it up and respond with dignity. We should not make the world even worse by trying to cash in on our personal setback at the expense of others.

The great success of the tort reform movement is its exaltation of the ethic of individual responsibility. The great failure of tort law's defenders is their inability to convince the American public that most tortious injuries are rights violations that harm society in general.

HOW THE MISSING PLAINTIFF THWARTS
THE PROMISE OF TORT LAW

As I set out to solve the mystery of the missing plaintiff, I did not think it necessary or helpful to prefer the ethic of rights over the ethic of individual responsibility. As I've already mentioned, I see little likelihood that our national injury problem can be solved by freeing tort law from the constraints imposed by tort reformers. I'd like to state as clearly as possible, however, why the reluctance of injury victims to press claims weakens the very foundations on which tort law's founders built their institution. The way our legal system works, a victim's decision to claim is the switch that sets tort law in motion. The mobilization of tort law, in turn, is meant to achieve certain highly desirable ends. For one thing, by requiring the injurer to pay for the loss, it is meant to provide *compensation*—the law "makes the victim whole again" and restores him or her as a productive member of society. In addition, damage awards are meant to have a *deterrent* effect for those tempted to make bad choices about the risks they impose on society. Furthermore, by requiring injurers to restore that which they have taken away from their victims, tort law provides an important moral and symbolic sanction, known as *corrective justice*. And some would say that tort law has yet another purpose. When the injurer is in the best position to purchase insurance or self-insure against injuries, imposing liability results in *loss distribution* across a broader population rather than forcing victims to absorb the entire loss themselves.

Tort law experts love to argue about which of these theories—compensation, deterrence, corrective justice, or loss distribution—is most important for addressing society's injury problem. But all of the theories depend on injury victims actually coming forward to assert claims. The victim's claim is tort law's sine qua non. If it turns out that claiming by victims rarely occurs, if most potential plaintiffs absorb their losses without confronting the injurer, then neither compensation nor deterrence nor corrective justice nor loss distribution can result. If most potential plaintiffs remain inactive, tort law's promise is thwarted. Its capacity to attain its own stated goals is undermined. If most tortious injuries never get close to a courtroom or a lawyer's office, then many landmark judicial decisions based on different assumptions about victims' behavior—not to mention countless law review articles and classroom discussions—will need to be revisited.

ECONOMIC AND CULTURAL EXPLANATIONS
FOR THE DOG THAT DOESN'T BARK

But, you may respond, the case of the missing plaintiff isn't that mysterious after all. There are two simple and obvious explanations for the absence of claims that make it unnecessary to devote an entire book to the search for answers. The first is that most victims don't bring claims for a very simple reason: the costs of claiming exceed the benefits. This *economic explanation* assumes that physical injury victims, like the rest of us, are rational people who weigh the potential benefits of lodging a complaint against the costs in money, time, and aggravation—and the uncertainty of outcome. According to this explanation, the unwillingness of most injury victims to claim reflects a considered decision that the possible payoff for action is simply not worthwhile in comparison to inaction.

The economic explanation for the infrequency of claims is useful in many ways, but it has one major problem—the assumption that injury victims are rational decision makers is probably incorrect. In hundreds of studies across many disciplines—cognitive science, behavioral economics, and psychology, to name a few—one finds very little support for the view that people engage in conscious deliberation and rational choice in the aftermath of a traumatic injury. On the contrary, researchers have convincingly demonstrated that most thought is nonconscious and far from linear and rational. And, as we shall see, nonconscious thought profoundly affects conscious thought. Even when we think we are making deliberate, rational decisions, we are guided—and very often misguided—by nonconscious and irrational cognitive processes. Besides, even if injury victims were rational decision makers, it's still not clear why a careful weighing of costs and benefits would so often result in a decision not to claim. Why should the benefits of inaction almost always turn out to be greater than those of claiming?

There is another "obvious" answer to our question that might appear to make this book's inquiry unnecessary—the *cultural explanation*. Culture, it is sometimes said, imbues claiming, litigation, and stoic self-reliance with particular meanings that lead people to value or disvalue them in distinctive ways. If we want to know why injury victims rarely assert claims, we need to examine social norms and practices. Culture, according to this explanation, leads people to forgo claims they might otherwise assert.

Although many chapters in this book will engage in cultural interpretation, I think it's a serious mistake to conceive of culture simplistically as an external force that somehow compels us to elect certain kinds of legal or nonlegal action. What's wrong with viewing culture as a kind of behavioral straitjacket that restrains most of us from making tort claims and suing? For one thing, the inactivity of injury victims is not confined to any particular culture but appears to be a global phenomenon.[17] For another, according to the prevailing view of American legal culture, citizens in our society tend to be *more* inclined to claim than others, not less. A well-respected writer has asserted that Americans are notable for their heightened expectation of "total justice," by which he means "a general expectation of recompense for injuries and loss."[18] If this claim is correct, if American culture tends to endow claiming and rights assertion with *positive* values, then sole reliance on culture to explain the infrequency of claims would seem to lead us up a blind alley.

And so, as we proceed with this investigation, I don't plan to abandon either the economic or the cultural explanations completely but to recognize that neither perspective alone can provide a simple answer. The existing frameworks for thinking about why we don't sue are simply inadequate. It's time to take stock of what is really known about injuries, injury victims, and the processes of cognition and decision that lead so many individuals to make no claim in response—even when their inaction may have disastrous results. If it is indeed worth asking why the dog doesn't bark, then we need to launch a new kind of investigation to uncover useful clues and arrive at plausible answers. That is the aim of this book.

THE PLOT THICKENS

The litigation of injury claims is a matter of great interest, not just to legal specialists but also to politicians and the general public. Tort law attracts the attention of Hollywood film studios as well as corporate managers. It is the subject of esoteric legal theory but also of highway billboards and TV commercials. Everyone has heard of tort law. Millions of us have watched *Runaway Jury* and *The Verdict* or read *A Civil Action*. Everyone has been annoyed by injury attorney jingles on the radio and has laughed at lawyer jokes (for example, describing his contingent fee to a client, the personal injury lawyer explained, "If I lose your lawsuit, I don't get anything; if I win your lawsuit, you don't get anything."). Exactly what tort law is and how it works may be a little less clear in people's minds. But about one thing they are certain—there is too much of it.

In the next chapter, I will examine more closely this "fact" that is so obvious to most Americans—that we are a hyperlitigious society. A closer look at the actual data about injuries, claims, and lawsuits will reveal that a rather different phenomenon cries out for explanation, namely, why so many injury victims take not a single step in the direction of tort law. Indeed, most of them never demand anything at all from their injurers. Why should that be?

Like Sherlock Holmes, we will attempt to solve this mystery step by step. After examining abundant research data about the infrequency of claims in injury cases, I will begin the search for clues in the true-life experiences and personal narratives of injury victims. I will ask what it actually feels like to suffer a serious injury, and how the experience might dampen one's enthusiasm for demanding compensation. I will then explore prevailing theories about the choice to make a claim rather than simply "lump" it (as in "like it or lump it"). In the process, I will sketch out a better model of how people make decisions when they have been injured, and I will use that model in the chapters that follow to investigate how the physical, cultural, and social contexts of injuries tend to foster lumping rather than claiming.

Few of us could match Sherlock Holmes's powers of deduction. But, in this case, we will discover many clues begging for attention. The crucial first step is to clear away the clouds of misperception and misinformation that have obscured the real question in this case. Once that question has been clearly presented and its importance explained, we should be able to focus on the behavior of injury victims that truly demands explanation. The effort will prove worthwhile. In the process of solving the mystery, we can encourage a reconsideration of the things Americans value and the things they feel they must simply endure. In our attempt to explain the silent suffering of our fellow citizens, we may discover the kind of people we really are.

Sociologists are not famous for the elegance of their prose, but surely one of their clunkiest expressions is "lumping"—derived from the rather surly admonition, "If you don't like it, you can lump it." The dictionary definition of lumping is "to put up with; resign oneself to; accept and endure,"[1] and this is more or less its social scientific meaning as well. A disputant with a valid legal claim who engages in lumping is one who absorbs the wrong rather than taking action against another party. As William L. F. Felstiner wrote in one of the earliest articles to discuss lumping as a form of legal behavior, "In lumping it the salience of the dispute is reduced not so much by limiting the contacts between the disputants, but by ignoring the dispute, by declining to take any or much action in response to the controversy."[2]

Lumping doesn't simply refer to not filing a lawsuit—it covers much more ground than that. It means, at least for purposes of this book, that the victim does not confront the injurer in any significant way to seek redress. It means that the victim makes no phone call to insist on compensation from the injurer or the injurer's insurance company. It means no use of third parties to demand a remedy—no lawyers, no mediators, no ombudsmen, no Better Business Bureau personnel, and no other go-betweens or would-be dispute resolvers. Injury victims who lump make no determined effort to shift any of the injury costs to the injurers or hold the injurers responsible for the harm. Instead, the victims rely on whatever resources—financial, psychological, and spiritual—they can muster on their own. Relying on one's own health and accident insurance or on government benefits are all forms of lumping.

Claiming is the opposite of *lumping*. In this book, claiming is defined as any effort by an injury victim to force the injurer to provide a remedy. Claiming may involve use of the law, but it may also occur through extralegal contacts with the injurer, either directly or through third parties. By this definition, filing a worker's compensation claim for an accident suffered in the workplace is *not* a form of claiming, since it does not involve a demand that the injurer pay compensation to the victim. Similarly, when victims of the 9/11 attack requested compensation from the September 11 Compensation Fund, they were not claiming by this definition, since they didn't insist that the injurers themselves provide a remedy to the victims.[3]

Those of us who teach tort law don't spend much time discussing lumping with our students. By ignoring the issue, we undoubtedly contribute to the impression that most victims of tortious behavior lodge claims. Each year, I ask my incoming first-year students to complete an opinion survey based on the beliefs or assumptions they bring with them to law school. Each year the students confidently opine that Americans rarely lump their injuries, frequently assert claims, and typically file lawsuits to vindicate their rights. Each year they are shocked to learn that these commonsense answers are completely wrong. A substantial body of research stretching back at least thirty-five years has established conclusively that lumping is not rare at all but is by far the *most common* response to physical injuries, that claiming occurs very seldom, and that litigation is extremely infrequent. The empirical research that produced these counterintuitive findings is of two different types: (1) research on people with injuries, asking how they responded to their mishap; and (2) research on people with grievances of many kinds, asking how they pursued their sense of being wronged. Both types of studies have led to a broad consensus among sociolegal scholars that lumping predominates among injured Americans. This chapter, then, presents step one of our investigation. It describes a body of research establishing beyond any reasonable doubt that the dog in most injury cases does not bark.

STUDIES OF LUMPING BY INJURY VICTIMS

Approximately nine out of ten injured Americans choose to lump rather than claim. That, at least, is the conclusion suggested by survey research that identifies injured Americans and tracks their post-injury behavior. The most extensive and widely cited national survey of this kind was conducted by Deborah R. Hensler and her colleagues at the RAND Corporation. They didn't study all injuries. They excluded fatalities and accidents that resulted in institutionalization of the victim in a long-term care facility. They also excluded accidents that resulted in illness, such as the use of dangerous or defective pharmaceuticals or asbestos products.[4] Some of the millions of injuries they didn't study will figure importantly in the later chapters of this book.

But if we focus for the moment on injuries the RAND researchers did study, we can see some very interesting patterns in the victims' responses. More than 90 percent did not make any claim against the injurer or its insurance company but

---

TABLE 2.1. Responses to accidental injuries in the United States

Action taken by injured person	Frequency (%)
Did not consider claiming	81
Considered claiming but took no action	10
Took some form of action	10
(dealt directly with injurers or their insurance companies or consulted an attorney)	
Hired attorney	4
Filed lawsuit	2

Source: Hensler et al. 1991 at 122.

---

simply absorbed costs themselves, got help from their own insurance, or at most filed a workers' compensation claim.[5] We have defined all of these responses as forms of lumping. The comparison of claiming to lumping by American injury victims appears in table 2.1.

It might be objected, however, that this overwhelming portrait of lumping in America is distorted, because it combines both minor and severe injuries. We shouldn't be surprised to learn that individuals who suffer trivial bumps and bruises respond passively. But surely, the skeptic might argue, most people who experience major harms do make claims, consult lawyers, and when necessary bring lawsuits. The RAND researchers, however, provide an answer to that objection.

It's true that those who suffer minor injuries are very likely to lump. Of that group, only 8 percent take any action at all, 5 percent consult a lawyer, and 3 percent actually hire a lawyer.[6] However, among those who suffer moderate (fractures or crushes) or severe injuries (life-threatening, long-term impair-

23

ments), the lumping rate is still surprisingly robust—78 percent among the moderate injury victims and 65 percent among the severe injury victims. These results are striking. *Two out of three victims of severe, life-altering injuries respond by lumping.*

The RAND researchers gained an even more fine-grained view of lumping by focusing some of their analysis on these exceptionally severe injuries. It seems that Americans are most inclined to lump severe injuries that don't involve work or automobiles. For example, Americans who suffered severe product-related injuries outside the workplace were found to lump 93 percent of the time. Severe slip-and-fall injuries on someone else's property (also nonworkplace) led to lumping in 90 percent of the cases. Severe injuries related to products that occurred on the job resulted in lumping "only" 84 percent of the time.

Lumping of severe injuries occurred least often in cases involving motor vehicle accidents. In those instances, lumping took place only 11 percent of the time, and 57 percent of the victims ended up hiring a lawyer.[7] We may speculate that motor vehicle injuries represent a special variation, since the involvement of police and contending insurance companies is so highly routinized that claiming in serious injury cases occurs almost without any effort by the injury victim. In all other contexts, however, when the victim must make a voluntary decision to press a claim or consult a lawyer, lumping is the overwhelming result even when injuries are debilitating and life altering.

The RAND study provides a benchmark figure for lumping by injury victims in the United States. Although it was published more than twenty years ago, its findings have not been challenged, and other surveys have produced similar results. For example, Richard Abel in 1987 argued provocatively that there were too few, not too many tort claims. His contention was based on data from numerous studies, including national surveys of unmet legal needs among the general population, comparisons of hospital records and insurance claims, data on workplace injuries from the Occupational Safety and Health Administration and the Bureau of Labor Statistics, the National Safety Council, and others.[8] From these studies, Abel concluded, "only a small proportion of victims take any action to redress their injuries."[9]

Tom Baker, after comparing litigated cases to hospital-based evaluations of medical errors in several different studies by medical experts, found that the rate of litigation was less than 3–4 percent. He concluded, "The vast majority of eligible patients do not sue. The idea that Americans are suit-happy, litigation-crazy, and ready to rumble in the courts is one of the more amazing myths of our time. It grows stronger with each piece of the by now overwhelming research showing that it is simply not true."[10]

STUDIES OF PEOPLE WITH GRIEVANCES

Unlike the studies of injury victims just discussed, a number of surveys begin, not at the initial stage of injury occurrence, but at a later stage when the victim has thought things over and decided she or he has been wronged. Grievance-based research begins with victims who already have a gripe with the injurer and asks them what they did about it. Consequently, this type of study inevitably omits a great deal of lumping that occurs before a clear sense of grievance forms in the victims' minds and overstates the percentage of cases that end up as claims or lawsuits.

Nevertheless, the findings of grievance-based surveys are instructive. A much-cited national study in the 1980s, for example, known as the Civil Litigation Research Project (CLRP), conducted telephone interviews with one thousand randomly selected households in five federal judicial districts across the United States. Respondents were asked, among other things, to report injury cases that had cost them $1,000 or more and in which they believed they were entitled to compensation. In this rather select group of costly injuries that the victims had already decided were worthy of compensation, 85.7 percent communicated their belief to the other party. The authors call these communications "claims," but there is reason to suspect that many of them failed to meet the definition of claim used in this book. That's because the authors do not state whether the discussion in such instances was initiated by a victim demanding compensation or by an injurer's insurance company trying to defuse the situation by unilaterally offering a settlement. If the victim never insisted on a remedy, then these communications were not claims as we have defined the term. Whatever the case may be, only 11.6 percent of the already aggrieved victims went on to consult a lawyer, and a mere 3.8 percent filed a lawsuit.[11] Even the grievance-based studies underscore how seldom injury victims initiate legal action.

LUMPING OF ACTIONABLE INJURIES

But survey research pointing to the predominance of lumping seems vulnerable to at least one very important objection: the injury statistics don't necessarily involve harms caused by an injurer who did something wrong. Tort law allows injury victims to recover damages only when there is another party—a defendant—who was negligent, marketed a defective product, or engaged in some other dangerous or proscribed form of conduct. Surveys such as the RAND study seem to jumble together tortious injuries with accidents that may have been caused by chance, by the victims themselves, or by injurers who did nothing blameworthy. If a case isn't "actionable," nobody would expect the injury victim to assert a claim and try to hold someone else responsible. If you slip on a wet rock in the river and break your arm, the failure to lodge a claim doesn't seem to be lumping at all but something rather different. Wouldn't it be better to exclude all of the nonactionable cases from the sample before concluding that lumping is the predominant form of response by injured Americans?

This is a pertinent objection, and the solution seems obvious. Researchers shouldn't survey all accidental injuries, just those that are actionable. But that's not as easy as it sounds! One of the primary purposes of a trial, after all, is to determine whether a claim is actionable or not. If it were simple to sort the actionable from the nonactionable injuries, there would be little need for courts and lawyers. Legal institutions exist in large part to interpret and judge the conduct of injurers and decide whether they have committed legal wrongs. Furthermore, the legal standards by which injurers are judged are not always stable. Courts continually engage in the process of expanding, contracting, and transforming definitions of "actionable" conduct as social norms and practices evolve. Marketing the dangerously explosive Ford Pinto was perfectly legal until a jury examined the claims brought by Richard Grimshaw and others and decided that Ford's conduct was tortious. After the verdict, we could say with confidence that Grimshaw had suffered an actionable injury; before the verdict, no one could be certain.[12]

Even injuries that seem to involve no one but the victim may be reinterpreted to cast responsibility on another person. We will have more to say about falls on staircases and the often invisible failure of engineers and architects to prevent them. For now, it's enough to note that there is no way that survey researchers can confidently separate the injuries that were caused by someone else from those that involved only the victim. The responsibility of another person—an injurer—is not a "fact" but a matter of interpretation, contestation, and sometimes artful lawyering. In this sense, too, it's impossible for a survey to draw clear distinctions between actionable and nonactionable injuries.

For these and other reasons, it's not as easy as one might think to determine how often injury victims engaged in lumping when they could instead have brought a successful legal claim. No matter how many carefully crafted questions the RAND or CLRP researchers might have asked about every accident they studied, they still would have found it extremely difficult to say which ones would have prevailed in court. Without the benefit of an actual trial, it would have been nearly impossible for them to restrict their analysis to those injuries alone and then to have counted the number of "righteous" cases that were lumped or claimed.

How then can we overcome this methodological problem and gain a more accurate picture of the frequency of lumping *in cases where the injury victim could have made a legitimate claim?* Michael Saks devised an ingenious solution when he was researching injuries caused by medical error. For this category of injury, there did exist a large group of cases that had already been evaluated as actionable or nonactionable by panels of neutral medical experts.[13] One might expect that the rate of claiming would rise considerably in the group of cases that these medical experts classified as actionable, but this did not appear to have happened. Although the available data didn't permit Saks to calculate an exact figure for rates of lumping and claiming outside the tort law system, he did determine that, of all the victims in cases classified by experts as actionable medical errors, only 4 percent hired lawyers and only 2 percent filed lawsuits. Remarkably, these figures are the same as those reported in the RAND survey for *all* types of injuries, both actionable and nonactionable. Saks gives us some reason to think that the rate of lumping might not differ greatly in actionable versus nonactionable injuries.

Nevertheless, no one can be certain about the rates of lumping for injuries in which, legally speaking, the victims deserved compensation from the injurer. We can't say for sure how a judge and jury would have decided each case, so we will never know whether an injured person has lumped a meritorious or a nonmeritorious case. What we can say for sure, however, is that lumping is by far the predominant response in American society and that the rate of lumping hovers around 90 percent in most studies, even for injury cases in which liability is highly probable. In short, research data overwhelmingly support the premise of this book—most injury victims engage in lumping, not claiming.

LUMPING AS DEFAULT IN AMERICA
AND ELSEWHERE

After four decades of empirical research, sociolegal scholars agree that claims are rare in injury cases and lawsuits even rarer. For example, more than thirty years ago Marc Galanter, one of the most respected figures in the field, observed that "a very large number of injuries go unperceived. . . . Even where injuries are perceived, a common response is resignation, that is, 'lumping it.'"[14] Haltom and McCann, in their important study, noted, "In general, empirical studies have shown that, for the vast majority of injuries, the injured demand no compensation—legal or other."[15] And Michael J. Saks, in his landmark article, concluded, "A tiny fraction of accidental deaths and injuries become claims for compensation; even known actionable injuries rarely become lawsuits."[16]

There is no credible evidence to the contrary. Study after

study has established that lumping is the default mode for resolving injury cases in our country. But is America different from other societies in its preference for lumping in injury cases? Although researchers have conducted parallel studies in other societies, comparisons are very difficult. Differences in social and legal arrangements complicate efforts to compare injury practices in Society A and Society B, and researchers often differ in their definition of key terms, including "injury" and "claiming." Furthermore, most studies begin with grievances rather than injuries, so it is nearly impossible to determine how many baseline injuries culminate in lumping versus claiming.[17]

With these caveats in mind, however, it is interesting to note that one study of responses to accidental injuries in England and Wales found a claiming rate of 10.5 percent, which is roughly the same as the American studies. Apparently, we do not differ greatly from our English-speaking counterparts in our extreme preference for lumping. On the other hand, Masayuki Murayama's study of Japan—which is usually characterized as a society that prizes harmony and avoids conflict—found that more than 82 percent of accidental injuries led to some contact with the injurer, and that 30.5 percent of these contacts resulted in disagreement![18] Does this represent a high rate of claiming? Does it mean that Japanese people, contrary to the usual stereotypes, far surpass Americans in their insatiable appetite for law? Not at all. The same study found that only 4.3 percent of all the Japanese injury victims consulted a lawyer, and a miniscule 0.4 percent filed lawsuits. The lawyer consultation rate is roughly similar to that in America, and the litigation rate is much lower. Although these figures are surprising, it seems safe to conclude from them that Japanese people may not lump nearly as often as Americans, but they are just as law averse. Maybe more so.

THE BIG PICTURE: MAPS OF
LUMPING AND CLAIMING

A highly influential article by William L. F. Felstiner, Richard L. Abel, and Austin Sarat[19] proposed a model that tracked the early stages of disputes from the precipitating incident to the emergence of a claim. Their map identified four stages in the development of claims, each of which could be applied to cases of physical injury as follows:

- *Unperceived injurious experiences.* Some injuries, such as an undiagnosed cancer caused by a negligent toxic exposure, are never known to the victim or are never perceived as injuries. They are viewed as part of the ups and downs of ordinary life. Victims who are unaware of their injuries would never assert a claim against the responsible party. They simply "lump" without even realizing they've done so.
- *Naming.* Injury victims may eventually realize they have suffered harm. They may "name" their injury—a crucial first step in transforming injuries into claims. For example, a cancer patient may learn that her condition is known as mesothelioma, an illness associated with asbestos exposure. But even when the victims have named their injuries, they don't necessarily connect them to the actions of an injurer nor view the injurer as having done anything wrong. Naming alone doesn't invariably lead injured men and women to assert a claim. Most still opt for lumping.
- *Blaming.* On the other hand, some individuals who realize they've been injured also take the next step. They blame their injuries on the wrongful actions of other parties, such as a negligent asbestos manufacturer.

Even so, no matter how resentful they may feel, most people choose in the end to do nothing about it. Blaming doesn't guarantee that injury victims will rise up and take action. The opposite is far more common, and lumping prevails even at this third stage in the process.

- *Claiming.* A relatively small number of injury victims do choose to lodge claims against their injurers. They do this in any number of ways, all of which involve voicing their grievances directly or indirectly to the injurer and asking for some type of remedy. When victims engage in claiming, they have left lumping behind. Claiming is the opposite of lumping. It's important to note, however, that claiming does not necessarily involve formal legal action. Victims can claim by making direct contact with the injurer with a phone call, a letter, or an e-mail, by invoking third-party dispute resolvers, or by relying on a representative or proxy. The use of lawyers and legal institutions is certainly a distinctive type of claiming, but it is not the only one.

The model developed by Felstiner, Abel, and Sarat suggests that injury cases may pass through several crucial stages before they "mature" into claims against the injurer. At each of these stages, there are ample opportunities to drop out, which is exactly what most people do. In other words, lumping is an alternative to each stage except the last and, as we have seen, it is the preferred option for most injured Americans. Figure 2.1 shows lumping as an ever-present possibility along the pathway to claiming.

One of the most striking characteristics of this model is how long and winding the road is from injury to claim—and we must keep in mind that there are a number of additional steps for the injury victim who decides to move onward to liti-

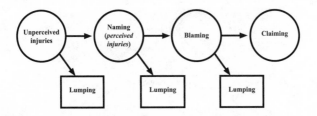

Figure 2.1. Lumping as alternative to naming, blaming, and claiming

gation. For example, the claimant who decides to sue must find and consult a lawyer. The lawyer must then decide to accept the case, and the injury victim must decide to hire him or her. For a case to proceed to litigation, the lawyer's initial efforts at settlement negotiations must fail. All of these steps must occur before a lawsuit is filed. And at almost every point, the injury victim still has the option to drop out and "lump it"—an option that is very often exercised.

The one word that best describes this general model is *attrition*.[20] Cases are constantly falling away from the process in much greater numbers than those that continue toward claiming, lawyering, and litigation. That is why many writers view the civil justice system, and in particular the handling of injury cases, as a pyramid with a very large base containing the many cases that arise in society. The pyramid has a tiny tip containing the rare and atypical cases that are litigated, adjudicated, and appealed, as depicted in figure 2.2.[21]

The pyramid model shows how lumping and nonjudicial dispute resolution diminish the flow of cases toward litigation. In fact, injury cases do not really "flow" into the courts, they merely trickle in. As we have seen, inaction by injury victims may account for as many as 90 percent of these cases from the outset, making the base of the pyramid more like a tomb and final resting place not just for Egyptian pharaohs but also for most injury cases.

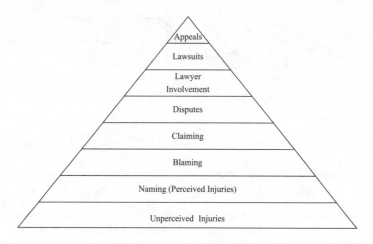

Figure 2.2. The tort law pyramid

The more I studied the tort law pyramid, the more I became convinced that we need to understand why such drastic attrition occurs at the earliest stages of the process. That is the goal of this book. The chapters that follow will trace the progress of my investigation. Before we begin, however, we should point out a few key features of the decision tree model represented by both the flowchart and the pyramid (they are both decision trees; the pyramid simply turns the flowchart on its side). The strengths of this model are also its weakness. Although the decision tree model has made it unmistakably clear that our civil justice system rests on a vast, largely unacknowledged substratum of incidents that never culminate in claims or lawsuits, it has also created some misimpressions about the post-injury behavior of victims. It may actually have obscured our understanding of why so many injuries end in lumping. A closer look at the decision tree model will clarify the features that ultimately limit its usefulness.

The decision tree model assumes *linearity* in thought and action. Injury cases in this model move in straightforward fashion from one stage to the next—unless they are lumped. The progression of cases from left to right (in the case of the flow-chart) or from bottom to top (in the pyramid) is mostly uni-directional and chronological. Although reverse movement is theoretically possible, research based on this model doesn't usually consider claims that jump nonsequentially—for example, from stage 3 to stage 2 or from stage 4 to stage 1. Rather, the decision tree model encourages researchers to think of cases as moving through time, step by step, from the first to last stages, unless they get stuck in a particular stage or drop out via lumping.

The dynamic force that propels cases along their linear path is a series of *decisions or choices* by the injury victims. Each stage, each level of the pyramid, contains a branching of the path. The victim stands metaphorically at each of these decision points in turn and selects one pathway or the other. The victim chooses whether to blame or not, whether to claim or not, whether to see a lawyer or not. Thus, victims move like pilgrims along a highway until they make a choice that terminates the journey. In the early stages, at least, termination of the journey entails lumping. But whether the choice is to stop or to move forward, a key feature of this model is the victim as a decision maker, as the active force that propels the linear movement from one stage to the next.

The third key feature is more subtle. It has to do with the concept of decision itself. On the whole—we will see that there are some exceptions—the decision tree model assumes that *decisions are the product of conscious and deliberate thought.* Some might go further and say that injury victims make decisions *rationally* by weighing the costs and benefits of each possible course of action. Injury victims know what their choices are, and they work their way through them by sensibly weighing the advantages and disadvantages.

The problem with the decision tree model is that each of these key factors—linearity, victim decision making, and conscious choice—is deeply flawed. Together, they construct an unrealistic image of injury and response that bears little relationship to injuries as they actually occur or to victims as they actually live, breathe, and cope with the dire circumstances in which they find themselves. Perhaps it is time to start over. We need to ask how real human beings experience physical injuries and how they respond to them. By going back to the physical and psychological realities of injuries, we may now begin to explain the predominance of lumping.

‖‖‖

It's all going . . . Darkness is gathering me into its arms.
Farewell wife, children, family, the things of my heart . . .
Farewell me, cherished me, now so hazy, so indistinct . . .
—Alphonse Daudet, *In the Land of Pain*[1]

We are not who we thought we were. America isn't a nation of trigger-happy litigators after all. We are a nation of lumpers. What can explain the reticence of injury victims to assert their rights? Why are Americans so reluctant to confront their injurers and insist that they make amends?

These aren't questions that usually capture the attention of torts professors or their students. In law school, we generally deal with cases in which injury victims do indeed assert a claim and sometimes dramatically expand the frontiers of tort law. We seldom acknowledge how rare and atypical these cases are. We don't study the very opposite of the landmark claims featured in the textbooks. How could we possibly teach our students about the far more typical instances in which injury victims respond to legal wrongs with passivity or resignation? Cases in which nothing happens—like *Seinfeld*'s fictional TV show "about nothing"—are unlikely to enliven classroom discussions.

To solve the case of the victim who lumps, I decided to begin at the scene of the crime—or, in this instance, the scene of the nonevent, the injury that doesn't culminate in a claim. Thus, the starting point in this chapter is the experience of injury itself. In our fascination with dramatic, high-profile tort cases, few of us ask what it actually feels like to be seriously injured. What is the thought process of the injury victim? Do the painful event and its aftermath generate ideas, emotions, and decisions that naturally lead to lumping rather than claiming? Perhaps we have taken injury victims for granted. If we were to listen to them more closely, we might find clues that explain why most injured Americans never pursue a claim.

IMAGINARY AND REAL LIFE INJURY VICTIMS

I've come to realize that the injury decision tree, which many of us cite in our research, is not helpful at all in conveying the lived experience of the injury victim. It conjures a highly unrealistic picture, something like this: The injury victim is convalescing at home. He lies in bed near a table full of medications. Perhaps his leg is suspended in traction or his arm encased in plaster. He thinks about the incident that caused his harm. After careful analysis, he decides that someone else was to blame, not himself, not fate. He sees a fork in the road ahead. Should he proceed down the path to the left by picking up the phone to demand compensation? Should he call his injurer? Should he claim? Or should he turn to the right and lump, having calculated that the amount he might receive would be too small a return on the time and aggravation it would cost him? He weighs this choice for many long days. He carefully assesses the costs and benefits of each course of action. And then he reaches a thoughtful decision . . .

But really? Does this scenario bear any resemblance to the messy, contradictory, nonlinear thought process of real people as they muddle through the devastating effects of a serious injury? It became more and more clear to me that this idealized image of the injury victim as intrepid decision maker was utterly false and highly misleading. When people suffer serious injuries, or even less serious injuries that cause pain and disruption, they don't behave at all like travelers journeying along a branching pathway. Few of them engage in anything like a series of deliberate calculations and considered choices.

Imagine instead an entirely different scenario, something toward the serious end of the injury spectrum. The injury victim has been traumatized by his accident. He is shaken physically and has suffered painful wounds, fractures, and disabilities. The structure of his life has collapsed. He is disconnected from familiar relationships and routines. He feels isolated, frightened, depressed, and confused. Lynne Greenberg, who was involved in a devastating automobile accident, conveys what a person actually experiences when suffering severe pain:

> I am in pain from the moment I wake up until the moment
> I go to sleep. On a scale of 1 to 5, my pain never falls below
> a 3 and will rise at some point to a 5 nearly daily and stay
> there for hours. These spikes are unrelenting, stare-at-
> the-ceiling, wait-it-out pain. Its sinews unfurling, the pain
> whips through the middle of my head. . . . Sometimes the
> pain is so intense that even the skin on my face, particularly
> around the eyes, hurts like a bruise. My eyes also burn
> and smart and sting. I would later learn that in scientific
> terms, one could describe my pain even more accurately
> as "retro-orbital," "holocranic," "halocephalic." In more
> emotional terms: Inescapable. Disabling. Punishing.
> Grueling.[2]

Greenberg's days are filled with medical appointments, with an endless search for the specialist who can help her, with efforts to keep her family life from disintegrating, and—most of all—with an hour-by-hour, even minute-by-minute, attempt to endure her excruciating pain and the fear and anxiety that accompany it.

Do injury victims tend to make carefully considered decisions about naming, blaming, claiming, and possibly litigation while their bodies are in agony and they are struggling simply to survive day by day? Do such options even cross their minds? How many injured people are capable of giving these matters their sustained attention or conducting a rational analysis of costs and benefits?

Another writer, Lous Heshusius, tells us that the aftermath of a serious injury can exile the victim to a new world where nothing but pain can be seen, thought, or imagined:

> When intense pain takes over, nothing else exists. There is only a spot, a point, a sharpened point of nothingness. And yet it is the only spot where one can still *be*. Where there is still life. Life without thoughts. Without emotions.[3]

Does it make sense to imagine such a person making rational choices about the merits of claiming and legal mobilization? This is an individual who feels stripped of thought, emotion, and language, whose consciousness has been reduced to a single "point of nothingness" that is pure pain. Models of lumping based on decision trees and flowcharts drain the painful experience of its reality. They erase precisely those qualities that make injuries injurious—the *pain and suffering* that are so fundamental to injuries that even tort law recognizes them and deems them worthy of compensation in the form of "general damages."

In order to understand why lumping is the predominant response of injury victims, it is essential to listen to the words of those who have experienced injuries and to consider their lives, thoughts, and emotions in the aftermath of trauma.

Their accounts remind us that real world injuries are quite different from the lifeless abstractions suggested by diagrams and charts.

EXISTENTIAL CHANGE

Perhaps the most immediate sensation of the injured person is the shocked realization of existential change. As Gillian Bendelow and Simon Williams observe, "[P]ain reorganizes our lived space and time, our relations with others and with ourselves."[4] People in pain form a new sense of their bodies and their very identities. According to Mary H. Wilde, "When illness or injury strikes, physical changes occur and people experience their bodies differently. . . . As they try to adjust to extreme bodily changes, they may feel separated from their bodies (disembodied) or overwhelmed by physical sensations (especially pain)."[5]

Injuries are not the only source of pain, but very often pain does accompany injuries. Bendelow and Williams tell us that injury victims suffering from pain can become strangers to their own body: "the painful body emerges as 'thing-like'; it 'betrays' us and we may feel alienated and estranged from it as a consequence."[6] In Jean Jackson's words, "Pain exiles sufferers from their own bodies, which surface as 'strangely *other.*'"[7] Amputated limbs still seem to be there in phantom form,[8] and injured limbs that are still attached seem to be missing or no longer connected to the body.[9] The body that was once so familiar seems entirely remade.

For some people, years may pass after a severely disabling injury before it becomes possible to regain a stable and positive personality.[10] Until then, injury victims may experience strongly negative personality changes that disrupt relations with former friends. As one interviewee reported,

At first, people noticed a big change in me. I mean, I was really depressed, with good reason. Maybe that's why a *lot of my friends* got scared and stopped seeing me; they couldn't deal with the big change they saw in my personality. I've pretty well got my old personality back now, and I have developed a whole new set of friends. It took a long time, but what a difference it makes to life.[11]

Injury victims in these accounts are not confident decision makers poised at a fork in the long road to litigation. Instead, they are individuals whose sense of self has been profoundly shaken. It is not even clear to them who the "decider" is, since their very identity has become strange and unfamiliar. They are virtual exiles from their own bodies, living in a new "land of pain," as they struggle to accept a transformed physical self.

STRUGGLING TO THINK CLEARLY AND ACT DECISIVELY

Unlike the mythical figure who makes carefully considered decisions about claiming and lumping, injury victims in the real world often find their thought processes profoundly compromised. In studies of individuals injured in motor vehicle accidents, as many as 50 percent suffered from posttraumatic stress disorder as well as depression, fear, fatigue, and headache.[12] Moreover, during the years immediately following such injuries, drivers reported heightened levels of "personal safety concerns, worries about driving, trait driver stress, exhaustion, and negative physical symptoms" as compared to drivers who had not been in motor vehicle accidents.[13] In other words, experiencing an injury produces changes in mind and body that are defined by greater levels of stress and fear, particularly with respect to the same activity—in this case driving—that led to the individual's injury.

The depression, disorientation, confusion, and anxiety experienced by injury victims can result from the trauma they have suffered, but it may also be a side effect of the treatment they receive. Pain medication and other strong prescription drugs can contribute to one's inability to think clearly. As Greenberg recalls, "Only much later would I realize that it wasn't the pain alone, but rather all of the medications I was taking that made it so impossible to read, lulling me into a cocooned cloudy haze, a cotton-balled insulation that dulled the pain somewhat but made it impossible for me to think coherently."[14] And Heshusius describes the effects of morphine on her thoughts and emotions:

[M]orphine brought on violent hallucinations at night. During the day, my mind was a dense fog. I moved in slow motion. There was a pervasive sense of being absent. I couldn't hold a thought. I started to substitute words, saying "Zuzuki" instead of "jacuzzi," "root" instead of "food." I started a sentence and couldn't finish it, but started another sentence instead.

The effects of pain medication on Heshusius's ability to think and speak coherently presented her with an impossible choice: "Do I want my mind distorted and have less pain, or do I try to put up with the pain so my mind stays clear?"[15]

Both the pain of injury and the side effects of palliation create fog, confusion, and altered psychological states. Clear thinking becomes a difficult challenge. Decisive action and follow-through may seem nearly impossible. Rather than traveling down a clearly marked path, the injury victim may feel lost in a dark forest.

SOCIAL ISOLATION

One of the most common consequences of serious injury is the loss of friends and acquaintances. Although we might expect friends to rally round and support those close to them who suffer harm, their reaction usually proves to be disappointingly different. Perhaps the suffering of a friend is too disturbing. Perhaps it reminds them of their own vulnerability and mortality. Perhaps it becomes tedious. Whatever the explanation, injury victims almost invariably find that their social network has drastically constricted. In Greenberg's words,

> As the months progressed, my social world also shrank.
> So many acquaintances, work colleagues, and fellow
> parents at our children's school seemed to vanish. . . .
> On the infrequent occasions when I emerged from my
> hermit's existence, acquaintances initially asked the
> usual questions: "How are you?" I would answer, "The
> same." "Any improvement?" "No." Then I would feel
> the silent judgment: what a bore she is. And, at the next
> near meeting, I would greet, instead of questions, a
> ducked head as the person scurried away from me. I
> was a leper or, perhaps, merely the accountant—
> predictable, vaguely distasteful, joyless. Who wouldn't
> avoid me?[16]

Bill Clinton told Americans he could "feel your pain," but it turns out that many of our friends cannot. Feeling another person's pain is harder than it sounds.

The injury victim kills the buzz and makes others uncomfortable. When recovery comes slowly or not at all, acquaintances find they have little to say by way of encouragement. In Erving Goffman's terminology, the injured person's identity is "spoiled." As Goffman brilliantly described, an injury or disability can profoundly affect interactions with others, who may view the injury "as just retribution for something he or his parents or his tribe did, and hence a justification of the way we treat him."[17] The awkwardness of social interactions can lead both "normals" *and the injury victim herself* "to arrange life so as to avoid them."[18]

Even worse, acquaintances may deny the reality of the pain and suspect the injury victim of exaggerating or malingering. Since pain cannot be seen, observers too often believe it simply doesn't exist. As Heshusius learned:

> Someone else's pain, then, can never be confirmed and is, therefore, often denied and always underestimated. These truths echo in the stories told by those in chronic pain who speak of doctors, employers, friends, and even family members who think the sufferer is exaggerating, who can't believe it can be all that bad.[19]

For individuals who are already traumatized, anxious, and depressed, how much more dispirited they must feel when they discover that their friends and acquaintances avoid them and may even suspect them of lying about their suffering. No wonder injury victims become complicit in the severing of their own social ties. No wonder they find themselves isolated from their usual sources of support and encouragement.

FAILURE OF LANGUAGE

In order to voice a claim, it's essential to communicate one's suffering to others. Yet those who have experienced serious injuries agree that this is extremely difficult to do—and perhaps it is impossible. Elaine Scarry has written eloquently about the incommunicability of pain: "Whatever pain achieves, it achieves in part through its unsharability, and it ensures this unsharability through its resistance to language."[20] Researchers consistently find that language fails the injury victim. As Jean Jackson has observed of patients suffering from pain:

[P]atients both pursue language—answers, names, definitions, meanings that promise reassurance and cures—and avoid it. Although they have found that language fails to represent their being-in-the-world, that promising meanings turn out to be siren-meanings, that their quest to be understood as pain-full beings remains unfulfilled, they also want to use language to escape that experience, that world. Although they report feeling profoundly misunderstood, pigeonholed, and categorized by everyday-world language, this is the language they continue to pin their hopes on.[21]

Based on her own experience with pain, Heshusius confirms Jackson's observation. She has found that the impact of pain renders her unable to express herself: "When a major pain attack hits, I cannot form words. Thought and language are wiped out. I cannot communicate."[22] Greenberg's experience was much the same: "[A]ll logic seemed to have fled and language to have abandoned me." Expressive language failed her, but so did her ability to comprehend what she heard or read: "I found myself unable to write a sentence or to read. . . . How could one perform an act that requires mental concentration when one had the biggest headache of one's life?"[23]

Those of us who study claiming, lumping, and litigation by injury victims have failed to consider the damage that traumatic pain can do to the victims' ability to communicate. An injury, particularly a painful one, transforms the identity of victims in ways that defy their powers of explanation. The language and logic of everyday experience no longer apply to this new existence. Injury victims tend to feel, initially at least, that they are no longer themselves, that they are disconnected even from intimate friends by the profound transformation that has occurred in their lives, and that their access to everyday life and its discourses are blocked by an inability to communicate their new reality. Under such circumstances, it is easy to understand why a severely injured accident victim wouldn't readily launch an effort to obtain a remedy. It's difficult to pursue a claim while alienated from self and friends and unable to rely on language to communicate one's new circumstances and needs.

SELF-BLAME

There is one more important difference between real world injuries and those that are modeled by flowcharts and decision trees. Astonishingly, real injury victims tend to blame themselves for their suffering, even when it seems obvious that their accident resulted from another person's wrongful act. And, to some extent, society supports this perverse tendency to blame the victim.

Modern tort law allows injury victims to recover compensation if their harm results *both* from the wrongful act of another *and* from their own contributory negligence. Blameworthy victims can receive a damage award reduced by the proportion of the harm attributable to their own carelessness. They aren't precluded from recovery altogether. In the real world, however, neither injury victims nor the general public think about contributory negligence this way. The almost-universal assumption is that when the victim does something wrong, she loses her right to demand that the injurer take any responsibility at all.

It may be surprising to learn that, even in our supposedly litigious society, self-blame typifies the reaction of many injury victims. Jean Jackson points out that one of the most common associations with pain and suffering is the idea that the injured person must have somehow deserved his or her fate: "The Latin root for 'pain,' after all, means punishment. In a just and orderly world, our reasoning goes, innocent people would not be

suffering like this, so something must be *wrong.*"[24] The association of pain with punishment tends to be shared by the victim
as well as the society that witnesses her suffering.

Considerable evidence points to the prevalence of victim blaming—the assumption that victims should have taken
greater care, that they somehow deserve the harm that befell
them, and that the injury itself was fated to happen or may even
have been a form of cosmic retribution.[25] As Gillian Bendelow
and Simon Williams observe, the religious roots of such assumptions are unmistakable:

> [E]xplanations for suffering may be linked to deeply
> entrenched religious or spiritual beliefs, even if an
> individual does not follow any particular faith, and
> punishment and self-blame are common themes. While
> these beliefs may seem inappropriate and even anti-
> therapeutic to the physician, they may nonetheless
> preserve a sense of self-identity for the sufferer in the
> face of the impersonal rationality which bio-medicine
> may seek to impose.[26]

Researchers in Sweden interviewed women with medically
undefined musculoskeletal pain and found that many had
"self-blaming ideas." They viewed their pain as punishment
for their own misdeeds and shortcomings.[27] Similarly, Richard
Schulz and Susan Decker interviewed individuals with spinal
cord injuries and found that a remarkable 43 percent blamed
themselves to some extent for causing their injury. Furthermore, 56 percent believed they could not have done anything
to avoid it.[28] Neither perception—self-blame or inevitability—
is likely to encourage the victim to view another party as the
cause and seek to hold him or her responsible.

In short, self-blame by injury victims—and by society at
large—is both irrational and widespread. It trumps other po-

tential perspectives. Even though the law would allow some compensation for the injury victim who did indeed do something wrong, the psychology of self-blame is far more powerful than the rule of law. The perception that injury victims are responsible for their own suffering seems to preclude any possibility that the injurer should be called to account. This is not a deliberate decision by someone making a considered choice between two forks in the road. It is not rational. It is beyond reason—or *before* reason. This sort of thinking occurs before reason can enter the picture and displaces it.

CONCLUSION

Because of all the factors we have examined in this chapter, the injury victim in real life appears to be quite a different person from the theoretical figure who systematically works his way along a branching path, deliberately choosing at each decision point between lumping and blaming, claiming, lawyer consultation, and litigation. Instead, from our exploration of the accounts of injury victims, we can see that the accident experience itself—and the sometimes arduous process of recovery—encourages lumping. Too often, we overlook the most obvious fact about many injury victims—that they are not emotionless, dispassionate decision makers but human beings who are in pain, whether their injury is serious and life altering or merely disruptive. The experience of pain and trauma triggers particular patterns of thinking and feeling, which include a sense of existential change and feelings of disorientation, confusion, depression, and anxiety. Serious injuries also engender social isolation, the failure of language, and the widespread tendency to blame oneself.

Responses to real world injuries are rooted in suffering and the failure of reason and clear communication, not in deliberation and careful choice. Moreover, as we will see in the next chapter, much of our understanding in this field needs to be completely reconsidered in light of research by cognitive scientists. We may have vastly overestimated the role of conscious thought in the making of decisions, even when physical pain is absent. Researchers now tell us that decision making is primarily a nonconscious or preconscious function. When we study lumping and claiming in physical injury cases, we have tended to ignore the role of the body in relation to the workings of the mind. As we shall see, human thought encompasses all parts of our physical being and not just in our brain. We have not asked the next question: what happens to our "embodied" thought process when the body has undergone physical trauma? Could this be another reason why most injury victims end up lumping rather than claiming? Investigating these possibilities will lead us even further from the image of the injury victim as a decision maker who journeys steadily and systematically along the branching routes mapped by a decision tree.

Chapter 3 described my initial steps toward solving the mystery of the reluctant litigant. It explored the actual experiences of real life injury victims rather than the idealized behavior of the Reasonable Person or the Rational Actor, who are the usual subjects of analysis. We learned that injury victims' physical pain and trauma tend to produce withdrawal, social isolation, confusion, impaired communication, and self-blame; and all of these reactions make lumping far more likely than asserting a claim against the injurer. If physical harms have such a pronounced effect on cognition and behavior, why is it that most analysts ignore their consequences and blithely assume that injury victims make balanced and rational decisions? It seems most of our ideas about lumping, naming, blaming, and claiming have been distorted by a failure to recognize that injuries—even when they're not life threatening—can shatter the victims' world and compromise their mental faculties, their social relationships, and their ability to formulate and pursue a strategy of action.

Perhaps the findings in chapter 3 are enough to close the case of the missing plaintiff. I would argue, however, that several important leads remain to be explored. The mind-body connection, in particular, cries out for closer examination. Chapter 3 points to a research literature demonstrating that human cognition is so rooted in the body that it's impossible to separate thinking and decision making from the physical self. If that's the case, the findings presented thus far have barely scratched the surface. There is still a need to extend the investigation and consider much more carefully the workings of the "embodied mind," particularly when the mind is part of a body that happens to be injured and in pain. The latest—and quite fascinating—research on the mind-body connection will prove extraordinarily helpful in explaining why lumping predominates over claiming in most personal injury cases.

THE EMBODIED MIND

The narrator of S. J. Watson's thrilling novel *Before I Go to Sleep*[1] awakens in a room she doesn't recognize. A strange man lies beside her in bed. She goes into the bathroom and sees in the mirror a woman she doesn't recognize, someone considerably older than she thinks she is. She has no memory of her name or her history. Each night when she goes to sleep she completely forgets what has happened to her that day. She keeps a diary but must leave it where she hopes she will find it the next morning, when she begins again from a blank slate.

As the story develops, Christine, the narrator, tries to figure out how she suffered the traumatic injury that caused this unique form of amnesia. She begins to question who her husband and her doctor really are. She comes to believe she was the victim of a vicious assault, though it takes her most of the book to figure out who did it.

Christine makes one mistake after another as she seeks to understand her injury and decide what to do about it. Her mistakes are greatly exaggerated by her medical condition, but they are not unique. Christine faces the same paradox as other injury victims—she must use her mind to understand and respond to the harm her body has suffered, but her mind has itself been affected by the injury. How can she view her injury through a lens clouded by the very experience she seeks to comprehend?

The mind doesn't operate independently of the body like a freestanding observer capable of surveying the damage, assessing the cause, and making sensible decisions about the ideal response. Cognition doesn't occur independently of our physical beings, and bodies are not merely vehicles to carry around our brains. The body is not a "thing" or object but "a seat of subjectivity."[2] Cognitive scientists tell us that mind and body operate together as a unified whole. One of the most important contemporary insights about human thought is stated succinctly by Daniel Kahneman: "[C]ognition is embodied; *you think with your body, not only with your brain*."[3]

What does it mean to "think with your body"? Humans live in an environment that provides a broad range of experiences. These are perceived through all our senses. Although we may feel that "thinking" is a purely intellectual process, it actually involves all our body systems. As Mark Johnson has observed, "Experience comes whole and continuous. . . . [C]ognition is an organic, embodied process of enaction in which the organism is dynamically engaged with its surroundings and is not separated or alienated from them. . . . We are . . . *in* and *of* the world."[4]

According to this view, the old distinction between mind and body doesn't help very much in understanding how humans experience the world, since cognition is a function of the body in toto. As Joshua Ian Davis and Arthur B. Markman put it, "having a body is not a state, but rather an active element of

53

cognitive processing."[5] It is a mistake to imagine that the typical injury victim suffers damage to the body and then, in effect, refers the matter to his or her brain for a conscious assessment and response. Instead, it is more accurate to imagine an organic interconnection of environment, body, and mind. Together, they register the event, interpret its meaning, and shape the next steps. All of this happens rapidly, seamlessly, and for the most part nonconsciously.

Christine's story illustrates how crucial it is to consider embodiment when we seek to understand injury victims and their cognition. But it also signals another equally important consideration. Throughout the entire novel, Christine must wrestle with an existential question—who am I, and what has this physical trauma done to the person I was before? To understand the meaning of injury, we must understand the self who suffers harm.

According to neuroscientist Antonio Damasio, what we think of as the self is actually made up of three interrelated components, which he calls the *protoself, core self,* and *autobiographical self.* The *protoself* consists of "primordial feelings" and images generated by the body's encounters with its environment. Working together, body and brain register contacts with the things around them. Different parts of the body "bombard the brain with their signals, at all times, only to be bombarded back by the brain and, by so doing, creating a resonant loop."[6] The *core self* is associated with subjectivity, with awareness of who we are and how we interact with our surroundings: "The core self, then, is created by linking the modified protoself to the object that caused the modification, an object that has now been hallmarked by feeling and enhanced by attention."[7]

After her injury, Christine's cognition appeared to be relatively unimpaired at the level of the protoself and the core self, yet something extremely important was missing. Although she was fully capable each day of registering her body's engagement with its environment and even understanding the nature of her interaction with people and objects around her, Christine was unable to construct an enduring *autobiographical self.* She couldn't recall past events or create a chronology of experiences that carried over from one day to the next. She had no sense of who she was and what she had done over a period of time longer than twenty-four hours. Each morning she awoke without any life story, and her autobiographical self had to start anew. There was no internal narrative, no running storyline that connected her past to her present. As Damasio notes, the autobiographical self "embrace[s] all aspects of one's social persona."[8] It coordinates our memories of countless experiences and encounters in a lifetime. It arranges them into a "coherent pattern" and makes these patterns available to the self for purposes of future engagements with the environment and for future action.[9]

The autobiographical self is made up of the things we know and think about ourselves, but it also consists of memories and impressions that are half-forgotten, completely mislaid by our conscious mind, or even repressed. In other words, the autobiographical self operates both consciously and nonconsciously. As Damasio puts it:

> [T]he autobiographical self leads a double life. On the one hand, it can be overt, making up the conscious mind at its grandest and most human; on the other, it can lie dormant, its myriad components waiting their turn to become active. That other life of the autobiographical self takes place offscreen, away from accessible consciousness, and that is possibly where and when the self matures, thanks to the gradual sedimentation and reworking of one's memory.[10]

This, then, is the lesson from cognitive science: Any consideration of the way humans respond to physical injury must begin with recognition of the embodied self. Even when an injury does not completely disrupt one's memory, as it did for the fictional character of Christine, it is still perceived and interpreted through the interplay of environment, body, and mind. This process, as we shall see, takes place at both the conscious and nonconscious levels. The injured self emerges as a new person with a new identity and a new autobiography. The injury to the body becomes deeply embedded in cognition, and it affects the thoughts and decisions that follow, often in ways we never fully understand.

Injury victims are not at all the two-dimensional figures of the diagrams and flowcharts described in chapter 2. They are not like consumers pausing in the aisle of a pharmacy to make cool and dispassionate choices among different brands of toothpaste. Many have suffered severe trauma. Many have been shaken physically and have experienced significant changes in their lives and relationships. The effects of these physical harms are not separate and apart from cognition, since the distinction between body and mind simply doesn't exist. The mind, too, has experienced the body's pain and trauma. The injury victim is a frail and fallible being, not a sensible utility maximizer.

Richard H. Thaler and Cass R. Sunstein have argued persuasively that when we seek to understand how law intersects life, we should remember that the relevant actors are Humans, not "Econs" (*homo economicus*).[11] Humans are flesh-and-blood creatures who usually make their decisions on the basis of impulse, mistake, bias, and distortion, and they may be completely unaware of the factors that determine their responses. By contrast, Econs are imaginary, theoretical beings, who think and act reasonably after careful analysis of costs and benefits.[12] Thaler and Sunstein suggest that we will be badly misled if we base our analyses on the assumption that the world is populated by Econs rather than Humans.

By focusing the investigation in this book on Humans and not Econs, and by acknowledging that all cognition is embodied, it may be possible to take a big step in a new direction. We may be able to understand what actually happens when real people suffer injuries. It would probably look something like this: After an injury, nonconscious interpretive processes begin to operate immediately. The harm triggers both an organic response and a cascade of images and ideas through which the individual makes sense of what has occurred. At the same time, the individual attempts to position this traumatic experience in the flow of the autobiographical narrative that constantly runs through one's mind, shaping both behavior and sense of self.[13]

This is not the scenario that most of us have generally assumed, but it is much more faithful to contemporary views of human cognition. Indeed, this alternative picture of the injury victim is just the first step. We have now begun to journey away from the shores of the rational actor toward a new continent inhabited by Humans rather than Econs. We still need to know much more about the person who suffers harm and how the embodied mind struggles to find meaning in the traumatic event it has just experienced. Fortunately, there is an abundant literature on human cognition that provides guidance.

THINKING ABOUT INJURIES

Contemporary researchers think a lot about thinking. One of the most renowned theorists of thinking is psychologist Daniel Kahneman, author of numerous books and articles, including the recent bestseller *Thinking Fast and Slow*. Kahneman received the 2002 Nobel Prize in Economics for his work on decision making. His brilliant writings offer many clues to the question this book explores.

Kahneman tells us that there are actually two kinds of thinking, which he calls System 1 and System 2. System 1 comprises the automatic processes that quickly and effortlessly generate the "impressions and feelings that are the main sources of the explicit beliefs and deliberate choices of System 2. . . . System 1 has learned associations between ideas . . . ; it has also learned skills such as reading and understanding nuances of social situations."[14] The "fast thinking" of System 1 prepares and shapes the more deliberate and effortful "slow thinking" of System 2.[15]

Kahneman makes clear that the division of labor between System 1 and System 2 is generally efficient. If humans engaged only in slow, deliberate, and conscious thought, our lives would grind to a halt. We need the rapid-fire automatic operations of System 1 to get us through the day. Most of our thinking, in fact, is nonconscious. This may contradict our most cherished assumptions about who we are and how our minds operate, but it is nonetheless true. We are aware of System 2 thinking and tend to assume—mistakenly—that it represents the entirety of our mental processes. Meanwhile, System 1 operates in obscurity, handling most of the cognitive work that needs to be done.

We imagine that we are rational creatures, but our sense of careful, deliberate choice is generally an attempt—not a particularly accurate one—to explain our thought process to ourselves after the fact. As another psychologist, John A. Bargh, has observed, we arrive at our perceptions and our actions nonconsciously, for the most part, and then try to "make sense of them in terms of those aspects of which we are consciously aware."[16] But we are kidding ourselves. Much of the time we don't really act rationally or even consciously at all, we just create a plausible story of rationality to satisfy our self-image.

Because we aren't generally aware of the enormous extent of our nonconscious cognition, we fail to realize how broadly it shapes our conscious thought. The aspects of our thinking that occur consciously and deliberately are, Jonathan Haidt writes, carried on the back of our nonconscious thought like a rider on an elephant. The rider has the illusion of control over the gigantic beast but is largely subject to its sometimes unfathomable whims:

> Automatic processes run the human mind, just as they have been running animal minds for 500 million years, so they're very good at what they do, like software that has been improved through thousands of product cycles. When human beings evolved the capacity for language and reasoning at some point in the last million years, the brain did not rewire itself to hand over the reins to a new and inexperienced charioteer. Rather, the rider (language-based reasoning) evolved because it did something useful for the elephant. . . . Reason is the servant of the intuitions. The rider was put there in the first place to serve the elephant.[17]

Fast, nonconscious thought not only predominates in human cognition, to a large extent it controls it. Our conscious self is just along for the ride. When we think we are making choices and engaged in decision making, we are usually just riding the elephant of nonconscious thought.

ERROR, BIAS, AND IRRATIONALITY

Psychologists sometimes ask their subjects to do very strange things. Lawrence E. Williams and John A. Bargh asked a group of unwitting volunteers to hold either a warm or cold cup of coffee in their hands and then assess the written description of another individual. Williams and Bargh found that the bodily experience of warmth influenced how some of their subjects perceived other people and led them to see "warm" interpersonal traits that weren't apparent when their hands were chilled by cold coffee cups. By briefly changing their subjects' bodies, Williams and Bargh could change their cognition.[18]

It seems that we really do think with our bodies, but our bodies can be tricked by mischievous researchers. If you want to sell someone a used car, you should begin by altering their physical condition. Hand them a warm cup of coffee, and they could become more trusting and receptive without even realizing it. Or, if you can get them to smile, their new bodily state may trigger a number of positive thoughts.[19] At the other extreme, we can only imagine how the painful, mutilated, and broken bodies of accident victims must affect many of their thoughts and decisions, no doubt for the worse. We do know for sure that transformations in one's body can predictably produce patterns of thinking that are far from reasoned, logical, and objective.

Our rapid and automatic thinking can be fooled, and its errors have ripple effects on our conscious thought. In fact, as I read study after study by behavioral psychologists, I sometimes had the impression that psych experiments are mostly an exploration of human fallibility, of our inexhaustible capacity to commit cognitive errors and arrive uncannily at mistaken judgments. Many, perhaps most, of these mistakes can be traced to the influence of nonconscious cognition on conscious thought; and we have seen that nonconscious cognition, in particular, is rooted in the body.

The pervasive impact of nonconscious cognition on conscious thought causes us to make numerous judgments that, as Kahneman puts it somewhat drily, "are not well described by the rational-agent model."[20] Although cognitive scientists may differ in their view of how helpful or harmful our mental shortcuts are, most would agree that they bear little resemblance to the sensible decision making of the mythical "rational actor."[21]

Conscious thought has many talents and virtues, but it is lazy. Effortful thinking is, well, effortful, and life is short. If there's an easy way to avoid the time-consuming and sometimes exhausting mental effort of conscious thought, our nonconscious cognition seizes on it. The mental shortcuts of the nonconscious mind can derail rational thinking in countless ways. When subjects are shown two incorrect statements, they prefer the one that appears in bold font. People tend to believe statements printed in bright blue or red and not those in green, yellow, or pale blue. They attribute positive meanings to gibberish words or phrases on the basis of "mere exposure" on repeated occasions, as compared to the negative connotations they perceive in similar gibberish that they've never seen before.[22]

Three types of cognitive bias can result from the effect of nonconscious thinking on conscious thought, even when we imagine ourselves to be engaged in sensible reasoning:

- Overconfidence. Our seemingly reasoned judgments may rest on an overly narrow foundation, but we feel quite sure of ourselves on the basis of the insufficient facts that we know (or think we know). We drastically underestimate the importance of what Donald Rumsfeld called "unknown unknowns."
- Framing effects. Our judgments are distorted by how facts are presented. We reach different conclusions, for example, if we are told that our chance of surviving an operation is 90 percent than if we are told that our chance of dying is 10 percent.
- Base-rate neglect. We tend to make judgments based on information about individual instances while ignoring all the general (base-rate) information that could help us put them into context and estimate whether they're really common or typical.[23]

The laziness of the conscious mind manifests itself in another way, what researchers call the "status quo bias." Human cognition and decision making are prone to inertia. People are biased in favor of staying with what they have, even when a rational balancing of costs and benefits might lead them to act in order to change their circumstances. Indeed, Thaler and Sunstein argue that the status quo bias is so significant a factor in human behavior that it can serve as the basis for "soft" policy practices, which they refer to as "nudging." Instead of mandating a particular behavior, they contend, the government needs only to designate the preferable choice as the default option and leave it to individuals to select other options that policy makers deem less desirable. Human inertia will then cause many to accept the officially preferred default rather than take the initiative to choose some other course of action.[24]

Does the status quo bias help to explain the inaction of most injury victims? Is it a clue to the predominance of lumping? Possibly, but applying the status quo bias to the behavior of injury victims is actually a bit tricky. Much depends on how the situation is framed.[25] When an individual suffers an injury, what exactly does he or she perceive as the status quo—the situation beforehand or afterward? The difference could be significant. If an injury victim understands the post-injury situation to be the status quo, then that fact alone could influence her to lump rather than act affirmatively to change her circumstances. If, however, she understands the status quo to be her healthy situation before the injury, then she may be more inclined to pursue a claim in order to restore the status quo ante and avoid suffering a loss.

Without further research, it's difficult to say which perception of the status quo predominates in the mind of most injury victims. It may be relevant to note, however, that in a much-cited article on status quo bias, Samuelson and Zeckhauser found that the inertia effect persisted even when a particular condition was *imposed*—as is the case for injury victims, whose loss was imposed by the injurer.[26] Even under those involuntary circumstances, the subjects tended to exhibit an "irrational" preference for leaving things as they were rather than making the effort to change them. It is therefore plausible at least to conjecture that the status quo bias operates to encourage lumping rather than claiming by injury victims.

CONCLUSION

The mind performs many amazing feats of cognition, but it is prone to biases and mistakes that arise without our awareness. We make judgments all the time, sometimes good and sometimes bad. We rarely remain in doubt. We take shortcuts, we commit errors, we substitute questions we think are easy for those that are truly difficult—and then we arrive at answers that don't quite measure up to the predicaments in which we find ourselves. It's not that humans are incapable of reason. Rather, our day-to-day thoughts and judgments can get derailed in many ways, and our powers of conscious, rational cognition are often subverted by our automatic, nonconscious thinking. We may strive to be Econs, relying on our superior powers of rational analysis, but in the end we are only Humans.

If we are to understand how injury victims really think about the harm they have suffered, how they analyze their experience and decide on a response, it's essential to consider this abundant research on human cognition. We must abandon the notion that a body receives harm and the conscious mind then sorts things out, weighs its options, and chooses the best or most cost-effective path to pursue. Instead, we must construct a different kind of model. We must imagine body and mind together experiencing and interpreting the injury. We must assume that the initial cognitive work takes place nonconsciously in ways that largely determine the conscious thought processes that follow. The next chapter will consider what this process of injury-related, embodied cognition might look like and how it leads so many injury victims away from claiming and toward lumping.

FIVE

THEORIES, MODELS,
        DOGS, AND FLEAS

||||||||||||||||||||||||||||||||||||||||||||||||||||||||||||||||||||||||||||||||||||||||||||||||||

That's fine in practice, but will it work in theory?
—Garret FitzGerald[1]

A professor must have a theory as a dog must have fleas.
—H. L. Mencken[2]

The case of the missing plaintiff has reached a turning point. Having learned a great deal more about how human beings actually experience physical injuries and how they think about them afterward, we can be quite certain that the old assumptions about victim behavior simply don't measure up. To put it bluntly, there's a huge gap between our theories of injury claims and the evidence of social science. Existing theories and models no longer seem to fit the facts. The problem isn't that the evidence is incomplete, although it's always helpful to have as much evidence as possible. The real problem is that we've taken the evidence we already have and assembled a fundamentally flawed picture with it. Before continuing the investigation, we need to step back, reassess, and propose an entirely new framework based on the best information available about human cognition, injuries, and decision making.

THEORIES AND MODELS

Constructing theories may seem an ivory tower exercise, an annoying and useless practice associated with fusty professors. But ordinary people rely on theories, too, whether they realize it or not. Theories are simply attempts to explain why we see certain patterns in the things we observe—and, some would add, to predict what will happen next.[3] Oddly enough, people don't generally take in data and then develop explanations to fit the facts. Instead, they start with their explanations—their theories—and then they tend to look for information that supports them while ignoring anything that doesn't. Psychologists call this tendency the "confirmation bias," and Daniel Kahneman tells us that it affects the thinking of experts as well as laypeople: "Contrary to the rules of philosophers of science, who advise testing hypotheses by trying to refute them, people (and scientists, quite often) seek data that are likely to be compatible with the beliefs they currently hold."[4]

Sherlock Holmes had probably not heard of the confirmation bias, but he was well aware of the tendency and warned against it: "It is a capital mistake to theorize before one has data. Insensibly one begins to twist facts to suit theories, instead of theories to suit facts."[5] But that is exactly what we do. We take in the facts that fit our theories, we filter out the ones that don't, and we constantly "twist facts to suit theories." That's why it's crucially important to recognize what theories we rely on when we deal with the facts—and to develop new theories when the old ones don't work anymore.

This book addresses the confusion associated with a popular but empirically unfounded theory about Americans and the law. According to this theory, our courts are flooded with lawsuits because injured people bring an inordinate number of claims for compensation against their injurers. This general theory has spawned a number of subsidiary theories that purport to explain American litigiousness. Let's call them *hyperlexis theories*.[6] According to these theories, the reasons for the astronomical rates of personal injury litigation range from unscrupulous personal injury lawyers to an unrestrained sense of entitlement, a uniquely American obsession with individual rights, a breakdown in traditional community norms and institutions, a me-first philosophy among the citizenry, and pure and simple greed.

The problem with these and other theories—which are widely shared by members of the public as well as talking heads and policy makers—is that they attempt to explain a social phenomenon that doesn't exist. As Sherlock Holmes would no doubt observe, this is "a capital mistake." Any theory, no matter how elegant, has little value and can cause a great deal of mischief if it ignores the facts. Because of the confirmation bias, we tend to ignore or discount all the evidence that contradicts hyperlexis theory, and we accept as gospel the dubious assertions that support it. But facts are facts. As we have already seen, researchers have demonstrated time and again that most injury victims—even those who have been severely harmed— are *not* litigious and generally lump rather than claim. Unfortunately, this evidence doesn't match popular preconceptions and is banished from the mind without careful consideration. There are sufficient contrary data to lead any self-respecting detective to follow Sherlock Holmes's advice and consider alternative theories that actually fit the facts, rather than simply ignoring—or twisting—the evidence. And yet, this rarely happens. Such is the power of theory in everyday life.

What is to be done? Before we can develop new theories about American law and culture that explain the actual reluctance of injury victims to bring claims against their injurers, we need to assemble the existing facts to correspond more closely to reality. A good place to start is with a second look at the models we use when we talk about litigation, lumping, and claiming.

A "model" is a representation—often a visual representation—of how a process works. It provides a "simplified representation of the real world."[7] Social scientists devise models in their research, but laypeople also go about their daily lives with models of reality in their minds. Theories are closely related to models. If a model provides a reasonably accurate portrayal of events and behaviors, it can help us devise good explanations—good theories—for why things happen as they do. Of course, a model must correspond to the real facts in order to be useful. If its representation of the world is based on erroneous or misleading evidence, it will simply produce more bad theory. The downward spiral of error, self-deception, and bad policy will continue.

Focusing now on the models used to represent the process of injury, lumping, claiming, and litigation, it appears that even the best and most insightful researchers have tended to rely on a *decision tree* model. Since many of us cite this model frequently to rebut hyperlexis theory, it's difficult to step back and critique it. Yet, the preceding chapters of this book should make us uneasy. The decision tree model doesn't fit very well with what we know about human thought and action. In fact, it has probably reinforced the false assumption that injury victims make rational and conscious decisions, that their responses follow a linear path, and that they behave as atomistic individuals. None of this is consistent with the evidence uncovered thus far in our investigation of injury claims. Despite the many contributions of the decision tree model, to the extent it portrays decision making as linear, rational, and individualistic, it is a flawed representation of reality. It has most likely distorted our understanding of injuries, claiming, lumping, and litigation, and it prevents us from considering why lumping occurs as often as it does.

This chapter proposes a very different model, a new visual

representation of the real world that draws on better evidence about how injury victims—Humans, not Econs—actually think and behave. It aims to start with the most salient facts we have discovered, then arrange them into a reasonably accurate working model, and thereby enable more robust theories about injuries and the law in American society. Instead of a decision tree model that looks like figure 5.1 or a pyramid model that rotates the decision tree ninety degrees and looks like figure 5.2, the model I am proposing does not assume linearity, rationality, or individualism in the decisions of injury victims. It does factor in the injury victim's physical and social environment, but not as mere "independent variables"—not, that is, as external factors but as elements intrinsic to the victim's "embodied cognition." The new model appears in figure 5.3, and the following section briefly explains it. The remainder of the book then explicates and applies the model in figure 5.3 in order to solve the mystery of the missing plaintiff.

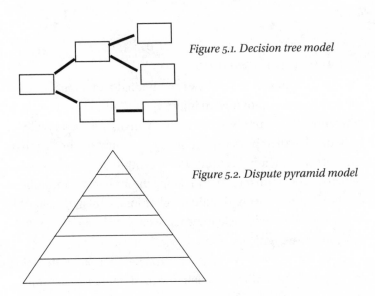

Figure 5.1. Decision tree model

Figure 5.2. Dispute pyramid model

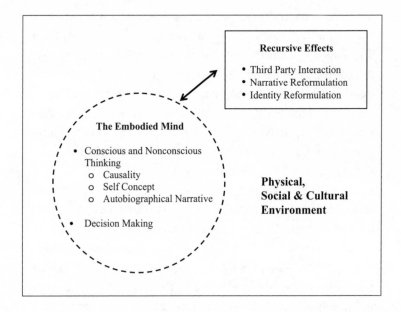

Figure 5.3. Alternative model of injury perception and response

FEATURES OF THE NEW MODEL
OF INJURY AND COGNITION

In figure 5.3, cognition is embodied and largely non-conscious. Movement toward injury victims' responses is multidirectional, not unidirectional. Individuals are organically embedded in their physical and social environment, not separate from it. And humans think and act within dense relational networks, not atomistically. By making these changes and substitutions in the conventional model of injury-related behavior, we should be able to theorize more effectively about why so many injured Americans lump rather than claim.

There are at least five reasons why the alternative model will improve our ability to explain the predominance of lumping among injury victims and, ultimately, to solve the mystery of the dog that doesn't bark. We describe them briefly here and then, in the chapters that follow, explore each of them in greater depth.

1. Both Lumping and Claiming Result from
Nonconscious Cognition as Well as Deliberate,
Conscious Decision Making

Both the hyperlexis theorists and many of their debunkers focus their analysis on individual actors and the decisions they make after being injured. They assume that individual decision making is the engine that drives the process, as injury victims choose each step along the pathway of naming, blaming, and claiming.

Of course, most commentators recognize that these choices can be influenced by external factors, including cultural norms, social values, social class, gender, race, and education. Neither side in this debate assumes that individuals decide matters in a vacuum. Nevertheless, both sides take it for granted that conscious decision making moves the process forward or brings it to a halt.

What's wrong with a model based on deliberate and conscious individual choice? The primary problem is that it fails to do what a model is supposed to do. It doesn't provide an accurate representation of the world. As discussed in the earlier chapters of this book, the best available research has established that individuals—especially those who suffer serious physical injuries—simply don't make decisions in this way. It's a mistake to assume that conscious or even rational decision making is the dynamic engine of dispute resolution, leading to either an excess or a scarcity of litigation.

The case studies in chapter 3 present a more accurate picture of the human response to moderate and severe injury. They portray injury victims whose perceptions and reason-

71

ing abilities have been seriously compromised. Dynamic is hardly the word to describe these damaged men and women. Injury victims are very often traumatized and impaired individuals, whose seemingly conscious choices are profoundly affected by nonconscious cognition. And, as we saw in the research summarized in chapter 4, conscious thinking in general is like a rider on an elephant, borne along by the enormous beast of the nonconscious mind. This picture is very difficult to reconcile with any model that implicitly relies on deliberate, conscious decision making as the force that propels things forward after an injury occurs.

In the alternative model represented in figure 5.3, injuries trigger a series of largely nonconscious perceptions and responses in the "embodied mind." These nonconscious cognitive activities may never be recognized or understood by the victim. Deliberate choices and actions are part of the model, but they aren't the most important factor and they don't set everything else in motion.

2. Cognition and Response Are Interactive and Multidirectional, Not Linear

The models we researchers use most often to depict the behavior of injury victims are linear and, as we have seen, typically take the form of a flowchart or pyramid. Cases proceed one step at a time from injury through naming, blaming, and claiming to lawyer consultation and the filing of a lawsuit. Propelled by the needs and desires of the injury victim, cases move from inchoate feelings that something is amiss to more focused, active, and institutional responses. The arrows generally point in only one direction. Although backward movement is possible— from claiming back to naming, for example—researchers have tended to give this possibility little attention. The model as applied is primarily unidirectional.

The alternative model of figure 5.3 rejects both the linearity and unidirectionality implied by conventional decision tree models. Injury victims do not proceed step by step in their thoughts and actions. As soon as people experience traumatic harm, their thoughts rush in many directions. Perceptions of painful injuries are immediately embedded in multiple complex cognitive frameworks. Images, explanations, and possible responses come all at once.[8] There is nothing linear about their thoughts or actions.

In the narratives of injury victims such as Lynne Greenberg and Lous Heshusius, we see constant movement back and forth. At times the injury seems all-consuming; at other times it is nearly forgotten. Their responses vary dramatically from total incapacitation and resignation to determined action. When they do respond, they may test several options at once, backtrack, give up, resume their former activities, pick up on a path they had previously abandoned, strive for a solution, arrive at a state of healing and acceptance, and sometimes suffer a relapse. Their responses are far from unidirectional.

The initial cascade of images and ideas triggered by the injury give the experience shape and meaning. They simultaneously engage different levels or aspects of the self—what Antonio Damasio calls the protoself, the core self, and the autobiographical self. Initial perception of the injury activates ideas about causation, blame, and responsibility. At the same time, the event is situated in the personal history of the victim. Things do not move steadily forward along a decisional pathway. Cognition of the injury can modulate the sense of pain, causing the severity of the injury itself to change in its perceived magnitude. Medical treatment and rehabilitation can also affect cognition, producing new understandings of what has happened and who or what might have caused it. Friends and family may become involved and can transform the injury victim's thoughts by contributing their own views and suggestions. Such changes in turn can produce new perceptions of the injury, its seriousness, its effect on the victim's life, and the level and type of response that might be appropriate. These interactive effects can continue for many years. It is not at all a neat and tidy sequence from step A to steps B, C, and D.

As individuals respond to the injury emotionally, medically, or by making practical arrangements, their own responses can affect their sense of pain and suffering. Decisions to blame, claim, or consult a lawyer may be followed by stress and relapse leading to inactivity or seclusion. It is impossible to map all the possibilities, certainly not in a simple flowchart. The post-injury experience is full of feedback loops, to-ing and fro-ing, starts and stops. A model based on linear, unidirectional responses pursued sequentially is simply inadequate to capture the realities of injury victims' thoughts and behavior. We need an alternative model that replaces the flowchart with a nonlinear representation.

3. The Decision Tree Is a Metaphor Created by the Nonconscious Mind and Not a Literal Map of How People Think about and Respond to Injuries

Although there's good reason to scrap the decision tree in favor of a less linear model, people sometimes do feel that they're moving forward along a pathway based on conscious choices made at crucial junctures. What is the source of this feeling? What is the origin of the decision tree model? George Lakoff and Mark Johnson offer a plausible explanation. The human mind, they tell us, functions by means of basic metaphors that structure thought and frame the perception of new experiences. These metaphors derive from what they call the sensorimotor domains. For example, from our sensory perception of physical and social experiences, we acquire the metaphorical understanding that "affection is warmth," "important is big," "more is up," "similarity is closeness," and "linear scales are paths."

Lakoff and Johnson argue that decision trees, which feel almost like real "things" in the world, are actually constructed out of two basic metaphors: (1) the metaphor of actors as travelers moving along a path; and (2) the metaphor that what is desirable in life can be expressed as a payoff, a quantitative increase rather than a decrease in well-being. Blended together in our minds, these two metaphors become the familiar decision tree:

> The achievement of a result is reaching a destination: If the result is desirable, you get money at the destination (a *payoff*). . . . The state in which you are making a choice is a location you are in. The possible courses of action open to you are possible paths that lead to destinations. A choice among courses of action is a choice among paths. The "rational" choice is the one that will allow you to get the most money or lose the least. . . . The next step is to take our spatialization in terms of locations and paths to other locations and visualize it metaphorically as a "tree," with the initial location as the "root," the trunk and branches as the paths, and the branching points as intersections of paths—places where one must make a decision as to which way to go. [9]

Lakoff and Johnson's analysis deconstructs the very model that has served as the basis for most theories about Americans' litigiousness—or lack thereof. The decision tree is merely a metaphor, a mental construct humans habitually use to imagine their world. We have made a fundamental mistake. We have used the decision tree as a literal map of human behavior when we should have regarded it as an object of study, a product of the very imagination we are trying to understand. The decision tree is no doubt interesting and important as a feature of the embodied mind, but it is not an objective analytic tool. That is, we shouldn't presume that the decision tree reliably charts victims' decision making. It isn't a fact-based model of reality.

Why should we be cautious about relying uncritically on the decision tree model? Why is it important to distinguish between its subjective and objective qualities? As Charles A. Lave and James G. Marsh pointed out many years ago, researchers' use of decision tree models injects certain presumptions and biases into their analyses. The decision tree is a "rational choice model [that] has a strong normative aspect." That is, it not only assumes that people act deliberately and rationally (which we have already learned is not usually the case), but it also tends to assume that they *should* make their decisions in a linear, stepwise fashion: "A normative model is one that tells you how to do something, how to behave in order to achieve a goal. . . . Normative models give advice, whereas descriptive models predict behavior."[10] Lave and Marsh emphasize that normative models do not necessarily describe actual behavior. They *might* be descriptively accurate, but that is not their primary purpose.

A hidden trap of the decision tree model in injury cases, then, is that it subtly imports the rational actor viewpoint without necessarily providing an accurate picture of the actual behavior of injury victims. If injured people do not usually behave rationally—and there is good reason to think they don't—then the decision tree provides only a particular unstated view of how they *should* act. It is more an ideological than an analytic instrument. It won't help us to accomplish our goal of understanding why so many injury victims end up lumping rather than claiming.

The alternative model of figure 5.3 does not assume that the decision tree provides a visual representation of objective reality. Instead, it attempts to take into account the largely nonconscious process—including the creation of metaphors such as decision trees—by which injuries are actually experienced and responses formulated.

4. The Mind and the Physical and Social Environment Are Organically Connected and Are Not External to One Another

Both hyperlexis theorists and their debunkers tend to view injury victims as separate from—but influenced by—their social environment. Peoples' thoughts and actions, in this view, are subject to external factors such as race, gender, social class, social norms, values, and cultural practices. At its most extreme (and simplistic), this perspective views human thought, choice, and action as dependent variables and culture and society as independent variables.

Nowadays, however, researchers question this binary view of people and their social environments. An extensive body of scholarship ranging from neuroscience to cultural studies strongly suggests that humans are organically linked to culture and society and not separable from them. The dualistic model of self and environment has now been widely challenged. Its critics contend that we should not think of culture and society as being "outside" the person but as part of him or her. Humans are quite literally the creatures of their environment, which leaves its traces in their minds and on their bodies. At the same time, human perception and behavior constantly shape the social environment and create the forms and practices that define it.

As Mark Johnson has observed, contemporary scholarship challenges not only the dualism of mind and body but also the related and equally untenable dualism of self and environment:

> There is no body without an environment, no body without the ongoing flow of organism-environment interaction that defines our realities. Once again, the trick is to avoid

the dualism of organism *and* environment, a dualism that
falsely assumes the existence of two independent entities,
each bringing its own structure and preestablished identity
into the interactions. Instead, we must think of organism
(or body) and environment in the same way that we must
think of mind and body, as aspects of one continuous
process.[11]

Johnson goes on to observe, "We are thus left with the somewhat counterintuitive idea that the body is not separate from
its environment and that any boundaries we choose to mark
between them are merely artifacts of our interests and forms of
inquiry."[12] In short, we should think of humans, to quote Maurice Merleau-Ponty, as "beings in the world." The human subject, in his words, "is nothing but a project of the world, and the
subject is inseparable from the world, but from a world which
the subject itself projects."[13]

The interaction of people and their social and physical environment creates the conceptual structures by which they interpret every experience and make each important decision—
including how to respond to a serious injury. The alternative
model of figure 5.3 therefore aims to avoid the dualistic view
of self and environment and instead to highlight their organic
interconnection. In this model, the environment is not external
to the self. The two are seamlessly linked and inseparable.

5. Interaction with Other People Is Key to Individual Cognition and Decision Making

The individual depicted in the decision tree model is a lonely
creature, a solitary traveler along a branching pathway. Although writers who rely on this model would undoubtedly acknowledge that friends, family, and coworkers could influence

choices to lump or claim, the model is essentially individualist in its conception. That is, the self is more or less autonomous and makes her own choices based on what she decides is best for her.

But we now know that the self does none of these things independently. The model depicted in figure 5.3 highlights the fact that the individual is constituted by his or her relations with others and not just influenced by them from time to time. Jerome Bruner writes of a self that is "distributed" among "the wider circle of people about whom any person cares or in whom he or she confides." This "complicit circle" becomes part of the self, "much as one's notes and looking-up procedures become part of one's distributed knowledge" and the self "becomes enmeshed in a net of others."[14]

The alternative model represents injury victims as embedded in relational networks that make them who they are. An individual's spontaneous interpretation of a harmful event is conditioned by prior association with a social group or is transformed by hearing how other people view such matters, particularly if they're close friends or relations. The injury victim's thoughts during the days and weeks following the injury are also shaped by others. Acquaintances can alter initial perceptions and decisions. The autobiographical self may, as a result of these interactions, begin to tell an entirely different story about the injury. There is, in other words, a back-and-forth aspect to the interpretive process that takes place over time and draws third parties into the victim's process of thinking about and responding to injuries.

Thus, injury responses reflect the various social groups and relationships in which the victim participates. If we are to explain the predominance of lumping, our alternative model must capture the crucially important interactions with others through which injured persons interpret experience, formulate the story they tell about it, and determine their response.

CONCLUSION: TOWARD A NEW MODEL OF INJURY AND RESPONSE

Is it possible to take all of these concerns and strictures into account in order to propose a different kind of model of injury and response? Can we create a visual representation that more accurately depicts the process we seek to explain? Figure 5.3 is, if nothing else, a step in the right direction. Many of the details will be explained in the chapters that follow. The most important aspects, however, should be immediately obvious:

- The decision tree, with its linear and stepwise characterization of injury perception and response, has been eliminated.
- There is no implicit presumption in favor of the rational actor.
- The model is descriptive and not normative.
- The mind is "embodied" and does not operate independently of the physical self.
- Cognition and action take place within the physical, social, and cultural environment.
- The self is embedded in the environment and is organically connected to it, as signified by the permeable, dashed line surrounding the self.
- Thinking is both nonconscious and conscious, both "fast" and "slow."
- Decision making is not an abstract or objective process. It is part of a continual stream of embodied subjectivity and is subject to bias and error.

- The self constantly interacts with third parties, such that cognition and decision are "recursive" in nature. Perceptions, narratives, and decisions are influenced by others and are reformulated as a result of those influences.

Figure 5.3, then, presents a model, a "simplified representation of the real world," that can serve as an alternative to the decision trees and flowcharts that have dominated discussions of claiming and lumping in injury cases. The complexity of human experience is not easily reduced to a single model. Figure 5.3 no doubt has its own shortcomings. But it is intended to portray more accurately how people actually experience injuries and respond to them. It deliberately avoids building in any particular normative preferences—that people *should* think rationally, they *should* maximize benefits and minimize costs, they *should* keep litigation in mind as a last resort if all else fails, they *should* conduct negotiations in the shadow of the law. Instead, it leaves open the possibility that all of these things may or may not actually occur. And it remains neutral as to whether the world would be better if they did.

Within this framework, we must now return to the experiences of real people, as reported by the best and most reliable researchers, to determine what actually happens when they suffer injuries. And, most important for purposes of this book, we must ask again why so many of them end up dealing with the consequences without making a claim against their injurer.

Figure 5.3 provides an alternative model of injury, cognition, and response that will serve as the basis for discussion in the remainder of this book. The chapters that follow will explore in greater detail the concept of causality (chapter 6), the physical environment (chapter 7), the social and cultural environment (chapter 8), and the injury victim's interactions with significant others (chapter 9). If this model proves to be a better and more accurate representation of the world, it can help to devise better and more useful theories about why we don't sue. And that, in turn, may shed important light on the role law does and doesn't play in addressing the problem of injury in our society.

SIX

CAUSATION, COGNITION,
AND INJURY

‖‖

To continue investigating why injured Americans rarely lodge claims, this chapter inaugurates the new model of perception and response presented in chapter 5. As we have seen, this model broadens the inquiry to include recent studies of cognition and the social context of injury, and it departs from the decision tree approach generally followed by researchers. Rather than confining analysis to the conscious thought processes and rational choices of injury victims, the model aims to include all the workings of the embodied mind in its physical, cultural, and social environments.

Where to start? The new model suggests countless applications, but one of the most interesting and potentially fruitful is the concept of causation, which is crucial to cognition and decision making. Evidence in this chapter will suggest that the universal tendency to make causal judgments—swiftly and nonconsciously for the most part and organically connected to the victim's environment—plays a key role in guiding most injury cases toward lumping. Causal judgments are a fundamental element of human thought. They are also a requisite element for the plaintiff to prove in every tort action. Somewhere in the spaces between neuroscience, legal science, and common sense, we may discover the origins of passivity, the reasons why so few injury victims decide to claim.

THE QUANDARY OF CAUSATION

Causation is a seemingly simple concept, but philosophers over the centuries have concluded that it's actually a can of worms. How hard is it to prove that A caused B? Well, a lot harder than you might think. Tort lawyers know they must establish that the defendant caused the plaintiff's injury in order to build a foundation for their legal claim—and that's not always easy to do. But causation isn't just a tort law concept, it's also a part of human cognition. As ordinary people conduct their lives, they continually observe and interpret their experiences. Human nature leads them, even without thinking about it, to impose order on what would otherwise be the chaos of random events. In doing so, they rely heavily on their ideas of causation. "B" occurred, we tell ourselves many times a day, because "A" *caused* it to happen.

Causation is therefore doubly relevant to our investigation of lumping in injury cases. First, it helps us to understand how the victim's own cognition operates to promote lumping. Where causation isn't obvious—or where injury victims don't perceive it at all—lumping occurs before there's even an inkling that a claim might be possible. Second, causation is also relevant to our investigation in the legal sense, because injury victims are less apt to bring claims if they or their lawyers think the judge will dismiss them on grounds of causation. Common sense tells us that claims become less likely as the chances for legal success dwindle. Judicial determinations of "no causation" can, moreover, reinforce cultural understandings that A really didn't cause B. Thus, negative legal judgments on the issue of causation can prevent future injury victims from even imagining that their misfortune was the result of someone else's action. There is a feedback loop from legal verdicts to individual cognition.

Let's begin with the first of these two ways in which causation can shed light on lumping—the role of causal inferences in the cognition of ordinary people who suffer injuries. How do injury victims think about causation? Everyday causal inferences may range from the trivial and obvious to the serious and highly controversial. When I sprain my ankle, an inner voice tells me that the *cause* was my own inattention. From that causal explanation, I conclude that next time I should watch more carefully where I'm walking. Aunt Rita prays every day for relief from pain and shortness of breath. She believes the neglect of religious rituals can cause illness, and piety can offer protection. Some families with houses near power lines believe that proximity to high-level electric currents causes cancer, though science has not established that such a risk exists. And some parents of children with autism have argued that the condition was caused by immunizations. Nearly all scientists dismiss these assertions, yet quite a few Americans firmly believe in a causal relationship and refuse to have their children vaccinated. In all of these instances, ordinary people make causal judgments to guide them day to day and, sometimes, through the most important events in their lives.

All of us constantly make causal attributions, but we are often completely wrong. If a neutral observer watched our minds at work, she might give us low grades for the quality of our causal judgments. The errors and biases we have already explored in the previous chapters are no less apparent when it comes to causation. Very often, for example, people mistake correlation for causation. They draw questionable conclusions about cold weather causing colds or marijuana causing heroin addiction. Although these mistakes are common, most of us understand the distinction between correlation and causation at some level and can even laugh at the failure to distinguish them. The rooster crows every day at dawn, but we would be amused if someone thought a barnyard animal could actually cause the sun to rise. According to humorist Tyler Vigen, the per capita consumption of cheese during the first decade of the twenty-first century correlates almost perfectly with the number of Americans who died by becoming tangled in their bed sheets. Yet few people would conclude that eating cheese can cause this unusual domestic tragedy.[1]

Many of our causal judgments cannot stand up to logic, and others vary with the perspective of the observer. But is it really possible, through objective scientific analysis, to winnow out all of these mistaken causal judgments, to purge our causal conclusions of irrational elements, and to arrive at the "true" cause for each event? Tort law is founded on the proposition that there are "actual" causes for injuries, and that no one—no matter how negligent or reckless her conduct—should be held liable unless the plaintiff has presented sufficient evidence of "causation in fact." It's a deceptively simple legal proposition: A's action, objectively speaking, either did or did not cause B's injury. Did A push the first domino and set off a sequence of events ending in B's accident? An omniscient observer would know the answer, it's usually assumed, and a jury must try to find it. To do this, tort law relies mainly on the "but for" test. It asks whether, without A's act, a preponderance of the evidence demonstrates that B would not have suffered harm. If the same injury would have occurred with or without A's wrongdoing, then A can't be considered the but-for cause and there can be no liability. The sun would rise whether the rooster did or did not crow in the morning.

That's how tort lawyers usually think about causation. But is causation really a fact that waits "out there" for us to either recognize or overlook? Or is causation more a mental construct, more subjective than objective? Is it essentially a habit of mind that connects A to B? That was the conclusion reached by the philosopher David Hume, who contended that we establish causal connections only because we repeatedly observe B in connection with A and conclude that B would not otherwise have occurred. Causation isn't something we can actually observe or detect; it's a matter of belief derived from experience.[2]

The now classic work of George Lakoff and Mark Johnson began to apply the insights of cognitive science to questions of causation. They suggested that humans comprehend the world through metaphors grounded in bodily experience. People understand states such as love, safety, madness, or depression as bounded locations—he is *in* love (or pain, or battle), they are *far from* safety, she is *on the edge of* madness, he is *in* a depression. We therefore tend to understand change from one state to another as movement into or out of such locations—he *went* crazy, she *fell into* a depression, they *entered* a state of euphoria. Therefore, we metaphorically understand causation as the force that moves us from one state (or location) to another.

Causal forces are also metaphors, and they originate in our everyday bodily experiences and movements, such as "pushing, pulling, hitting, throwing, lifting, giving, [and] taking."[3] These movements become mental templates, deeply embedded in our cognition, that we apply to all kinds of changes, which we interpret in terms of cause and effect:

> FDR *brought* the country out of the depression. The home run *threw* the crowd into a frenzy. That experience *pushed* him over the edge. The stock market crash *propelled* the country into a depression. The trial *thrust* O. J.'s attorneys into the limelight. . . . The United States *dragged* its allies into a commitment to the Gulf War.[4]

87

In short, Lakoff and Johnson argued that we understand causal relationships in the world through embodied concepts that are common to most humans. It's not always easy to say whether a cause "actually" exists or whether we merely perceive a causal relationship because of the way our metaphorical apparatus operates.[5] If we understand that Event A did cause Event B, it's probably because the connection between these two events (or "states") lends itself readily to metaphors we carry in our minds and customarily use to make sense of our life experience. If we fail to perceive a causal relationship, it's probably because the relationship between Events A and B doesn't match up very well with our preexisting store of metaphorical frameworks.

To characterize our everyday perception of causation as metaphorical takes us a long way from tort law's rule that injurers should be held responsible only if there's proof of an "actual" causal relationship between the defendant's misdeed and the plaintiff's harm. If Lakoff and Johnson are right, then injury victims do not view causation as an objective, rational observer would and as the law requires—at least not at the moment the harm occurs. Rather, people who suffer injuries interpret their mishap metaphorically. They ask—often swiftly and nonconsciously—what *force* caused the movement from a state of health or wellness to a state of pain and suffering. The answer to that question may be far from scientific and may even seem fundamentally misguided, yet it matters a great deal. The subjectivity of the injury victim can determine whether he or she connects another party to the injury—which is the critical first step toward blaming someone and bringing a claim. And we know that our initial perceptions can exert a profound effect on all the cognition that follows, both conscious and nonconscious.

HOW PERCEPTIONS OF CAUSATION
PRODUCE LUMPING

If the injury victim never perceives a causal connection to a potentially culpable actor—if he or she does not view someone else as exerting a force that led to a harmful outcome—then lumping will probably result. It's the subjectivity of the victim that really counts when it comes to lumping versus claiming, not whether the victim's perception of causation is objectively right or wrong. We need to ask, then, what factors might prevent victims from perceiving that someone else caused their injuries. The discussion that follows will outline five different ways in which the human construction of cause and effect can lead injury victims in the direction of lumping rather than claiming.

1. Lumping Because Causation Is Unknown

The failure to perceive a causal connection between an injury or illness and a probable source may result from a lack of information or knowledge. Cancer patients in the town of Hinkley, California, thought their illness resulted from bad luck until Erin Brockovich persuaded them that Pacific Gas and Electric was the actual cause. Initially, cancer sufferers in the town drew no causal connection because they were unaware of PG&E's pollution or its possible health impact. Later, thanks largely to the efforts of Erin Brockovich, they perceived PG&E as the cause of their misfortune, even though experts continue to question the causal connection that Brockovich (later portrayed by Julia Roberts in a Hollywood film) identified. "Unknown unknowns" can result in lumping by individuals who are simply unaware that a particular causal interpretation is possible.

Similarly, people who suffer from multiple sclerosis (MS) in one of America's so-called MS clusters may have no idea what has caused their condition—because scientists themselves are uncertain. Does MS originate in the wrongful conduct of other people, such as industrial polluters? Is it caused by cigarettes? Is it caused by diets high in animal fat or low in seafood? Is it merely the result of living in a northerly latitude, where less sunlight causes humans to produce less vitamin D?[6] Or are MS clusters completely random and not associated with any particular cause? Claims brought by MS patients against polluters or tobacco companies are extremely rare. Most choose to lump their illness simply because no obvious causal connection to a wrongdoer is known to them or to medical experts. Causation in the case of MS is an unknown unknown, and lumping is the result.

Humans are often reluctant to accept causal uncertainty, despite Voltaire's admonition to the contrary ("Doubt is not a pleasant condition, but certainty is an absurd one").[7] Surprisingly, many injury victims prefer to blame themselves rather than remain in doubt about the origins of their misfortune. Dan Coates and Steven Penrod speculate that victims who blame themselves "may be motivated by the human need to maintain perceived control," since self-blame allows them "to feel that the cause of some negative outcome can be directly manipulated by us."[8] Whatever the reasons for self-blame when causation is unknown, it typically leads victims to lump their injury rather than lodge a claim.

Sometimes life simply overwhelms us with its complexity. Injury victims can't figure out why misfortune has singled them out, nor can experts provide the answer. If we don't understand what caused our harm, if a potentially culpable cause has somehow been hidden, or if we resolve causal uncertainty by pinning the blame on ourselves, it never occurs to us to bring a claim for compensation.

2. The Link between Morality and Causal Judgments

In tort law, the issue of causation is supposed to be kept entirely separate from the issue of culpability. The defendant can be the worst person in the world, but tort law should not hold him liable unless the plaintiff can also present proof of a causal link between the defendant's bad actions and the plaintiff's injury.

In real life, however, concepts of causation are often conflated with questions of moral responsibility. People's perceptions of cause and effect can be strongly influenced by their judgments about the wrongfulness of the alleged injurer's conduct, even though the two questions are logically unrelated and should be considered separately. Janice Nadler's research demonstrates that our preconceptions about the moral character of the injurer are likely to influence our inclination to blame him or her for a mishap occurring. A person of good character is less likely to be blamed for an injury than a person of bad character in identical circumstances. According to Nadler, "We make blame attributions spontaneously according to how strongly negative our gut reaction is; then we validate our blame assessment by tuning evaluations of causation and intention accordingly."[9]

Social and cultural concepts and values become entangled in many complex ways with perceptions of injury causation and responsibility. In fact, our ideas about good guys and bad guys in society can lead us to launch a search for concealed causes, on the one hand, or to ignore glaringly obvious causal connections, on the other. For example, if a cancer patient believes that American factory owners should be held more stringently accountable for environmental pollution, she may search widely for a cause of her illness that connects it to toxic exposure from manufacturing plants. If, on the other hand, the same cancer patient is less concerned with pollution and is predisposed to think that most illnesses arise from people's spiritual or dietary imbalances, then she will be more likely to conclude that her illness occurred randomly or was even caused by her own perceived failures. In that case, lumping becomes the probable outcome.

These findings about the conflation of moral blame and causal attribution should come as no surprise to tort law specialists. In a classic article written more than fifty years ago, Wex Malone observed that causal relationships are not mere facts that can be established simply by producing evidence. Rather, they are "acceptable deductions" that are "drawn for a reason."[10] One's underlying purpose invariably shapes the conclusion that A caused B to happen. For judges as for laypeople, the blameworthiness of the defendant's conduct—and the policy benefits of holding a defendant liable—lead illogically to a greater likelihood of perceiving a bad person's action to be the cause of harm as compared to the very same conduct by a good person. In law, as in life, it's nearly impossible to separate our moral judgments from our causal attributions. Neither is prior to the other. Causation and morality shape one another in the human mind no matter how hard we try to keep them separate.

Thus, injury victims are not likely to perceive causal connections to their injurers in *all* cases but only in that subset of cases in which they deem the injurers morally blameworthy. If they make no such moral judgment, if they have a high regard for the neighbor whose incinerator belches toxic smoke or for the automobile company that sells them a dangerously defective vehicle, then they are less likely to draw a causal connection to the harm they've suffered. And, in those cases in which no causal inference arises, lumping will almost certainly result.

3. Cosmologies of Cause and Effect

Ideas about causation are embedded in worldviews that vary dramatically across social and cultural settings. Causal images and concepts in New York City are not necessarily shared by people living in the rural American South or the Pacific Northwest; and people in the United States may hold understandings of causation different from those of their counterparts in England, India, or Japan. Our causal judgments come not only from physical metaphors of bodies moving and acting in space but also from our religious, philosophical, scientific, and other perspectives that explain why bad things happen.[11] These broader cosmologies of cause and effect encourage some individuals to lump injuries that might otherwise have led them to lodge a claim.

The relationship between belief systems and causal attribution is easier to spot in cultures different from our own. Consider the following example from my own research in Thailand, based on an interview with a thirty-eight-year-old vegetable farmer named Thipha. She was involved in a serious accident while riding behind her husband on a motorcycle. Thipha offered not one but a series of causal explanations to account for her injury. Each cause drew on a different religious or philosophical framework. First, she cited a malevolent ghost that waited by the side of the road and obscured the vision of the oncoming driver. The ghost was associated with a nearby slaughterhouse, a haunted place of death. Second, she explained that she and her husband had accumulated bad karma when they tilled the soil and unwittingly harmed the tiny creatures that lived in it. Bad deeds cause suffering, if not in this lifetime then in the next: "Those creatures, whatever they were, we injured them without killing them. . . . That bad karma attached itself to us." Unlike the animist belief system associated with the roadside ghost, the karmic explanation was rooted in Buddhist concepts of cause and effect.

But Thipha pointed to other causes as well. A third was her failure to heed warning signs or premonitions. Her husband was uncharacteristically irritable and reckless that morning. He complained of a splitting headache and drove too fast. When Thipha warned him to slow down, he answered ominously, "Oh, are you afraid to die?" These signs should have alerted Thipha and her husband that their stars were in decline and their fortune at low ebb. They should have stayed home or exercised special care, but they ignored the astrological warnings and proceeded to the site of the accident. A fourth cause of the injury was negligence, but in a very particular sense of that word. Thipha assumes that injuries can arise when both parties—injurer and victim—lack mindfulness, or *sati*, which is another concept associated with Buddhism. In a world of careless actors, such as the oncoming driver who crossed over the center line and struck them, people have to guard against harm by being mindful at all times. The negligence of the other driver was therefore counterbalanced by the negligence of Thipha and her husband.

Two qualities stand out in Thipha's extraordinary causal narrative. First, the cultural environment offers multiple causal explanations, all of which tumble together in Thipha's account at the same time. Second, all of these causal explanations ultimately point away from the other driver and toward Thipha and her husband. Despite the other party's negligence, Thipha viewed herself as the root cause of her own injury. It's no surprise, given the version(s) of causality she drew upon, that she in effect lumped rather than claimed. When the other driver offered a token payment of only 3,000 baht (then approximately

$75), she and her husband accepted without hesitation. In light of the way she perceived causation, such a concession was all but inevitable.

But that illustration comes from a very different country on the other side of the world. Is it really possible that a similar cosmology of cause and effect could lead injury victims in the United States to lump rather than claim because of their worldviews or belief systems? Randolph Bergstrom, for one, makes that argument. He contends that a worldview favoring lumping predominated in New York City in the late nineteenth century. Predominant ideas about injury causation "rested in tradition, especially in self-sufficient individualism and a distaste for the strife that litigation expressed."[12] In the early twentieth century, however, Bergstrom contends that a fundamental change in thinking about injury causation became evident:

> What emerges is a public changing its mind about the cause of and responsibility for accidental injuries. The new ideas moved the citizens of New York to see their own injuries as consequences of the acts of other people who were often removed by time and space from the site of injury. The ideas also made those remote other people responsible for their acts.[13]

Another type of traditional worldview prevailed among long-time residents of a rural Illinois county I studied in the late 1970s.[14] Valuing self-sufficient individualism above the assertion of legal rights, local farmers and business leaders in "Sander County" believed that the primary and most important cause of injuries was usually a lack of care by the injured person. This view of causation was contested by some of the newcomers to the community but remained strong enough to persuade most injury victims in Sander County to lump rather than claim. In short, Americans, like Thai villagers, may indeed adopt worldviews, including beliefs about cause and effect in injury cases, that encourage lumping rather than claiming.

Some writers go even further. They argue that Americans' religious faith not only does but should lead injury victims to view causation as a barrier to claiming. From this perspective, claiming is actually irreligious. Douglas H. Cook, for example, argues that a "faith-based view" of causation would lead victims to see their injuries as part of God's plan, except in extreme cases where the defendant clearly sinned by choosing to disobey God.[15] If the cause of injuries is God's will, or the sinful behavior of the victim, then lumping is the only acceptable—and Christian—response.

Some jury experts, such as David Wenner, base trial strategy on the assumption that devout jurors do adopt what Cook describes as a faith-based view in injury cases. Wenner advises plaintiffs' attorneys to avoid empaneling jurors with "strong religious beliefs," since he has observed that such individuals tend to resist the conclusion that the defendant is the true cause of a plaintiff's injury: "[T]hese jurors believe that what happened to plaintiff is God's will or part of some divine plan, and the whole matter is preordained. The jurors often believe the rewards come in the next life or heaven. A belief like this renders moot and makes it unnecessary to file a lawsuit."[16] To the extent this advice is based on Wenner's actual experience with American jurors, it further exemplifies how Americans' worldviews and religious beliefs affect perceptions of causation and can lead them to view claiming as an inappropriate response to injury.

4. Historical Periods in Which Theories of Causation Suppress Injury Claims

As Bergstrom's study of causation in New York City suggests, popular views of causation are not static but tend to shift with changing circumstances. Whenever and wherever causal links to the wrongful acts of others become hidden or suppressed, lumping becomes the predominant response to injuries. Consider, for example, a seemingly simple causation case from 1920, *New York Central Railroad v. Grimstad*, which introduces the topic of tort law causation in some first-year textbooks.[17]

Angell Grimstad had made an odd career choice. Although he couldn't swim, he was hired by New York Central Railroad to serve as captain of a barge, the *Grayton*. Perhaps one attraction of the job was that he could spend much of his time with his wife, Elfrieda, who was onboard the day he drowned. According to Elfrieda's testimony, the *Grayton* was bumped by a tugboat while moored in the Erie Basin of New York Harbor. She was alone in the cabin, felt the collision, and hurried to the deck. Looking for Angell on one side of the barge, Elfrieda saw nothing and crossed to the other side. There she spotted him in the water approximately ten feet from the barge with his hands in the air. She ran back to the cabin, retrieved a small line, and returned to save him, but by then her husband had slipped below the surface.

Whatever thoughts Angell might have had about causation he took with him to his death. But we do know that Elfrieda, who became the administrator of his estate, decided that the cause of the fatal injury was New York Central Railroad's failure to provide adequate lifesaving equipment. In any event, that was the position taken by her lawyer, who made the unusual decision to sue Angell's employer for negligence. Elfrieda Grimstad's wrongful death case succeeded at the trial court level but was reversed on appeal. The United States Court of Appeals for the Second Circuit overturned the verdict because it concluded that what Elfrieda viewed as the cause of Angell's death—the absence of safety equipment—was not the cause at all! He drowned because he fell into the water and couldn't swim, not because of the railroad company's negligence. Without sufficient proof of causation, New York Central Railroad couldn't be held liable.

The *Grimstad* court never questioned the jury's finding that New York Central Railroad had been negligent in failing to provide adequate safety equipment. How then could it have concluded that New York Central did not cause Angell's death? As Elfrieda Grimstad frantically searched for something—anything—to throw to her drowning husband, she must certainly have thought that the lack of a life buoy or an adequate lifeline was the reason she was helpless to save him. What kind of thinking could lead a group of elite judges to conclude otherwise? Judge Ward's opinion criticized the trial judge for allowing the jury to engage in "pure conjecture and speculation." He wrote,

> [T]here is nothing whatever to show that the decedent was not drowned because he did not know how to swim, nor anything to show that, if there had been a life buoy on board, the decedent's wife would have got it in time, that is sooner than she got the small line, or, if she had, that she would have thrown it so that her husband could have seized it, or, if she did, that he would have seized it, or that if he did, it would have prevented him from drowning.[18]

In this passage, Ward and his fellow judges describe the hypothetical rescue of Angell Grimstad as it might have taken place had New York Central Railroad not been negligent.[19] That is, they applied tort law's traditional "but for" test to the facts of the case. They found that at each small step along the way—obtaining the life buoy, throwing it far enough, Angell's grasping it—things might have gone wrong. Therefore, it was impossible to say whether the presence of safety equipment would have made any difference. The finest life buoy in the world might not have saved his life. But what Judge Ward claimed to know for certain was that Angell drowned because he couldn't swim. That, according to Judge Ward, was the true cause of his death.

"There is nothing whatever to show" that New York Central Railroad caused Angell Grimstad's death. Well, nothing except common sense! Isn't it obvious that barges without life preservers are more likely to be associated with drownings than those with safety equipment, even when crew members do know how to swim? The causal connection seems so clear to a modern reader that this 1920 opinion looks like a transparent attempt to protect railroads from liability through a micro-analysis of what might have happened if the defendant had not been negligent. But this is how judges in that era thought about causation in injury cases. Or at least some of them did. There were other drowning cases from the same era in which courts reached different conclusions. For example, compare the *Grimstad* opinion to the more expansive view of causation expressed by Judge Learned Hand in the case of *Zinnel v. U.S. Shipping Board Emergency Fleet Corporation. Zinnel* involved a seaman swept overboard on a ship that, like the *Grayton*, lacked adequate safety equipment (a protective guard rope):

> Nobody could, in the nature of things, be sure that the intestate would have seized the rope, or, if he had not, that it would have stopped his body. But we are not dealing with a criminal case, nor are we justified, where certainty is impossible, in insisting upon it. . . . Considering that such lines were run for the express purpose, among others, of protecting seamen, we think it a question about which reasonable men might at least differ whether the intestate would not have been saved, had it been there.[20]

If courts were free to adopt either perspective on causation—the restrictive view of *Grimstad* or the expansive view of *Zinnell*—how can we explain the proliferation of decisions like *Grimstad* in the late nineteenth and early twentieth centuries? Most writers agree that the growth of American industry during that time was accompanied by a body of law that tended to protect railroads, factories, and other business corporations from liability for the increased number of injuries they caused. Causation was particularly useful in this effort. Even when proof of negligence was incontrovertible, many judges held that damages needn't be paid because the causal connection was too speculative, the causal chain too attenuated, or the number of competing causes too great.[21]

Grimstad's injurer-friendly view of causation was not adopted by every American court. Causation is a site of contestation in each historical era. But during times when the restrictive perspective tends to predominate, it can undoubtedly influence potential injury victims as well as judges. A few prospective plaintiffs, people like Elfrieda Grimstad, always seem to resist the spirit of the age and press claims against those whom the law appears to protect. But many others internalize the era's restrictive understanding of causation, or they sense the hopelessness of challenging it. Unlike Elfrieda Grimstad, these more realistic souls abandon any thought of bringing a claim. In this way, legal theories of causation in particular historical periods can exert an influence the moment an accident occurs and during the weeks and months that follow. The prevailing doctrine of causation shapes the thoughts of injury victims and their families and confirms their inclination not to bring a claim for damages. The emergence of restrictive views of injury causation at such times can significantly increase the likelihood of lumping over claiming.

5. The Enduring Influence of Restrictive Views of Causation

The legal doctrine of causation does not always favor injurers over their victims. To the contrary, some contemporary American judges have crafted novel and expansive theories of causation that have allowed plaintiffs to recover in cases involving DES, lead-based paint, medical errors, and other situations in which conventional proof of causation is nearly impossible. Nevertheless, the influence of the defendant's viewpoint on the development of tort law has remained significant since the mid-nineteenth century, if not before. To the extent their views have prevailed, claims by injury victims have been reduced and lumping has predominated.

Why is it that injurers have the capacity to shape contemporary tort law? In certain ways, the impact of potential tort defendants on legal doctrine may seem surprising. In the criminal law field, for example, we wouldn't expect those who injure others to have the most influence on doctrinal development and make it unlikely the courts will hold them accountable. Judges and lawyers sometimes revise the law to benefit criminal defendants, but the wrongdoers themselves don't represent an influential lobby group. Why, then, do civil wrongdoers have the ability to shape rules of causation that can insulate them from liability even in cases in which they've been found negligent?

Part of the explanation surely lies in the unequal social status and power of injurers and injury victims in America. Marc Galanter has pointed out that torts are one of the few forms of litigation in which "one-shot" plaintiffs, who tend to be "have-nots," sue wealthier "repeat-player" defendants.[22] Most tort defendants have deep pockets—otherwise personal injury lawyers wouldn't take the trouble to sue them. But tort plaintiffs are usually people of modest means and lower social status.

Injuries are not equally distributed across all social groups. Poor people are more exposed to risk,[23] often at the hands of wealthy individuals with sufficient resources to launch harmful activities or enterprises. Tort law is unique in this regard, involving claims by persons lower on the social totem pole against defendants who are higher up. Moreover, as "repeat players," potential defendants are more inclined to play the long game, anticipating future disputes in ways that one-shotters cannot, in order to strategize in advance for favorable rules.

Not surprisingly, "haves" tend to have narrow views about causation and responsibility for injuries. Since they are far more likely to end up as tort defendants and not as plaintiffs, the "haves" tend to endorse views of injuries as inevitable, nobody's fault, or the result of the injury victim's own carelessness. How likely is it that their views of causation will prevail? We would normally expect persons with more status and power to have a greater capacity to shape social and legal norms, both in local communities and at the state and national levels. Although the legal winds can shift direction from time to time, whenever the haves' perspective predominates, causation of injuries tends to be viewed primarily in terms of the victim's responsibility or even some divine plan. And when causation is conceptualized in these terms, lumping results. It's illogical to hold other people or companies accountable if they're not perceived as the real cause of the harm, and it may even seem immoral to do so.

To the extent the cultural and social environment reflects these ideas, the restrictive view of causation becomes more familiar than the expansive view. It takes on a greater sense of legitimacy, even in the thoughts of injury victims themselves. Such ideas about the cause of injuries become linked to the metaphors of causation that are constantly at work in our cognition. When an injury occurs, the mind consciously and nonconsciously seizes upon causal images that are immediately accessible and uses them to frame the experience.

Having identified a cause, moreover, we are irrationally reluctant to let go of it. We do not carefully weigh alternative explanations or consider new insights that might alter our perspective on causation. We tend to continue our search only for evidence that confirms the initial causal judgment and to screen out evidence that might contradict it. Once we have settled on a causal story, we tend to stick with it.[24]

CONCLUSION

We began this chapter with a simple premise—victims are likely to lump their injuries if there is no causal link to someone else's wrongdoing. But the plot thickened almost immediately. The existence or absence of causation is notoriously difficult to determine, because in a great many cases there is no objective test. Causation is more a habit of mind than a phenomenon of nature. The subjectivity of causation led us back to insights explored earlier in the book. We asked again how humans actually think about their experiences and make them seem coherent. It turned out that an important part of cognition involves making causal inferences, which we do constantly, even without realizing it. Why did an event happen? It happened, we tell ourselves, because A caused B to occur. Perceptions of causation enable us to make sense of everyday life.

If injury causation is indeed a phenomenon of the embodied mind, then our perceptions are subject to the biases and errors discussed in the previous chapters of this book. We view causation through a subjective lens. If the lens is clouded by self-blame or tinted with particular philosophical or religious beliefs, these factors may obscure causal connections that would otherwise be apparent. And where causation is absent, lumping is the likely result. Moreover, since cognition connects the individual to his or her environment, societal views of causation—sometimes influenced by judicial decisions—can loop back and shape the subjectivity of injury victims. Injurers often represent powerful sources of cultural production, so their views about injury causation are pervasive in society and are very likely to shape perceptions, even those of the victims themselves. When injury victims view causation in the same terms as their injurers, it is far more likely they will lump than claim.

The individual who has suffered an injury explains to himself and others what has happened—and why. His story of the injury draws freely on concepts, norms, and values from the broader social and cultural environment. Ideas about causation are integral to telling the story of the injury and formulating an appropriate response, and causal judgments can make either lumping or claiming seem an obvious course of action. But other features of the environment can also contribute to the decision to lump or claim. In the chapters that follow, our inquiry turns to the physical, social, and cultural environment to explore more broadly the many factors that explain why lumping is overwhelmingly favored by most injury victims.

SEVEN

THE PHYSICAL ENVIRONMENT
OF INJURIES

‖‖

In Carl Reiner's satirical film *The Man with Two Brains*, the character played by Steve Martin falls in love with a still-living brain in a jar, voiced by the irresistible Sissy Spacek. Discussions of injury victims sometimes give the impression that their minds, like that of Spacek's character in the film, are disembodied, pickled in preservative, and perched high on a shelf where they can observe events and make decisions at a safe remove from the physicality of real life. The alternative model presented in chapter 5 explicitly rejects this view. It regards the embodiment of the mind as an essential aspect of cognition. Equally important, however, it encourages us to ask how the embodied mind engages with its physical and social environment—as brains in bottles cannot. That is the focus of the discussion in this chapter and the next.

In this chapter, we ask how injury victims' thoughts are shaped by the objects and constructed features of the world around them. Although people tend to take the physical environment for granted, I'll suggest that its human-made aspects are actually laden with significance for injuries. If we critically examine the way humans create their surroundings and give meaning to them, we may discover deeply rooted assumptions about harms that are natural or inevitable as opposed to those that are unnatural and worth complaining about. It's only by exposing these assumptions that we can understand why and under what circumstances lumping becomes the predominant response to injury. This process of naturalizing injury can explain why a great many claims are never brought.

In the discussion that follows, we will consider a range of physical settings and objects and their relation to injury perception. In some instances, the nature of the physical environment reinforces the perception that the injury was natural and not the product of wrongdoing. In other instances, people may conclude there was no injury at all. And, in still other cases, it may be fully apparent that the injury was the product of a deliberate decision to expose others to the risk of injury, but the decision is associated with customary practices and doesn't seem blameworthy enough to justify a claim against the injurer. All of these variations, and others besides, emerge from an investigation of numerous objects and arrangements in our everyday environment, including stairs, chairs, and automobiles—as well as keyboards and a cup of hot coffee.

STAIRS

It should have been a day of celebration, not misfortune. On a bright February morning, ninety-one-year-old Luz Marina Montesinos arrived with her husband at the East Fiftieth Street entrance of St. Patrick's Cathedral in Manhattan to attend a special mass. Their daughter had arranged the invitation after hearing that World Marriage Day 2007 would celebrate couples married more than sixty-five years. Luz and her husband clearly qualified; they were approaching their seventy-second anniversary. No better site for the celebration could be imagined. St. Patrick's, constructed between 1858 and 1879, is one of the most famous and beautiful historic landmarks in New York City. Each year more than 5 million people visit, and more than 2,400 masses are celebrated there. Invitation in hand, the family began to climb the steps to enter the cathedral.[1]

By her own daughter's description, Luz Montesinos was a stubborn and independent woman. She told her husband to ascend the stairs ahead of her, because "she didn't want to be helped. She wanted to do it by herself." Since there was no handrail, Mr. Montesinos steadied himself against a wall as he went up. Their daughter followed behind him, and Luz took up the rear. She didn't brace herself against the wall and apparently proceeded without assistance of any kind. As she reached the second step, she fell and suffered severe, disabling injuries. At the time, she wasn't sure why she fell. There was nothing on the surface of the steps that could have caused the accident.

Luz Montesinos became one of the 1 to 2 million Americans who fall and suffer injuries on stairs every year, causing thousands of deaths and costing the public more than 10 billion dollars annually. Elderly people are especially vulnerable to such accidents. Approximately three out of four fatalities on stairs involve Americans aged sixty-five or older.[2] There was nothing particularly unusual about Luz's accident except her subsequent decision to bring a lawsuit against St. Patrick's Cathedral. Despite the huge number of stairway accidents each year, litigation is extremely rare, probably occurring in fewer than 1 percent of the cases.[3] Why should this be so? Injuries like those suffered by Luz Montesinos raise yet again the question why lumping is so prevalent in American society.

In the previous chapter, we saw that the *why* of injuries is crucially important. Victims' cause-and-effect explanations can lead them to attribute their suffering to someone else's wrongdoing, to fate, or to their own personal failures. Ideas about causation, according to Lakoff and Johnson, originate in the movement of the body in space, in the acts of pushing, pulling, lifting, and exerting force to produce change. From these formative experiences of humans moving about in their physical environment come the building blocks of our injury perceptions and our inclination to lump or to claim.

But the *where* and the *how* of injuries also have an important bearing on the attribution of responsibility to someone else. In this chapter, we consider the spaces through which people move as they interact with their surroundings. How are those spaces designed, and what objects do people encounter in them? To a large extent, though not entirely, humans make their own physical environment. But the physical environment also makes us who we are. The architecture of the spaces in which we live shapes our identities and imbues our experiences with particular meanings. Humans made the steps outside St. Patrick's Cathedral; but the steps also helped to make Luz Montesinos the human being she was—a woman who had to struggle to enter the church and someone subject to a heightened risk of falling.

People tend to take their physical environment for granted. Many of the spaces in which they live seem natural to them, rather than the product of human choice and design. Walking among the buildings, streets, and sidewalks of New York City seems much like a stroll among trees, lakes, and mountain paths. In the city, as in nature, we tend to take our physical surroundings as "given." But very often our physical environment is the product of human intention and is designed in ways that can either facilitate or constrain movement and can increase or decrease the likelihood of injury.

Stairways, like those at the entrance to St. Patrick's Cathedral where Luz Marina Montesinos fell, provide a particularly apt example of a taken-for-granted feature of our physical environment. The ability to move between lower and higher locations seems a natural part of life, and stairs are simply how we do it. Of course, there is nothing natural about stairs— they are an entirely human creation (although stair-like formations may exist in nature on hillsides or mountain slopes). Viewed from one perspective, stairs enable movement from one level to another; but viewed from another perspective, they make it more difficult or prevent it entirely. For persons with limited motor skills or for wheelchair users, stairs are among the most challenging and dangerous barriers they face in daily life.

It could be said that the million-plus annual stairway injuries result merely from the architect's initial decision to use the technology of the stairway rather than a ramp, escalator, or elevator (although these alternative technologies may produce their own share of injuries). But that's not how people generally think about stairway injuries. They don't blame the architect for failing to design a one-story structure or for incorporating stairs instead of ramps. Instead, people explain most stairway injuries as accidents that inevitably accompany human movement from place to place. They consider it normal—and perhaps even acceptable—that some of us occasionally trip and fall. If a few unlucky individuals fall down stairs, it must be the fault of their own physical shortcomings or carelessness. The tendency to blame the injury victim for preventable harms has been nowhere more apparent than in stairway accidents, and many safety engineers used to join this blame fest.[4]

It may be surprising to learn that engineers and ergonomics specialists now recognize that the risks associated with stairway accidents are not inevitable and can actually be significantly reduced—not necessarily by using alternative technologies but by designing the stairs more safely. As Patricia L. Jackson and H. Harvey Cohen observe, "From a review of our data and prominent stairway safety literature, we have found that many personal variables and external stairway characteristics may not play as great a role in stairway accidents as previously thought."[5] Victim blaming has obscured the culpability of architects and engineers for creating unnecessary risks. It is now known that accidents are less likely if stairs are designed with broader treads and shorter risers, and accidents can also be prevented by ensuring that treads and risers are regular rather than uneven in dimension.[6] From an engineering point of view, the most significant cause of injury on stairways—because it is the cause that is most amenable to risk reduction—may not be the victim's carelessness, age, frailty, or disability, but the design of the stairs themselves: "The findings . . . suggest that anyone who investigates stairway falls should use an ergonomics-based systems safety approach. This study indicates that stairway users are too often blamed for injuries that result from stairway and environmental factors."[7]

Why, then, did Luz Montesinos fall on the stairs of St. Patrick's Cathedral? An ergonomics expert might have concluded that she suffered injury not just because she was old, infirm, and stubborn, but because the stairs were unnecessarily dangerous. As it turned out, they had one of the features most likely to cause injuries—uneven height. At the place where Luz Montesinos attempted to climb the stairs, the first rise was only four inches above the ground, but the remaining steps were six and one-half inches high. Under such circumstances, falls such as hers were highly predictable—and preventable. But who would think to blame St. Patrick's Cathedral for her accident? The beautiful and popular neo-Gothic structure seems an integral part of the natural environment for New Yorkers, not the worldly creation of potentially fallible architects and engineers. Furthermore, its identity as one of the country's most famous religious buildings would seem to place it beyond blame or reproach. Given the choice, few observers (including judges or jurors) would side with Luz Montesinos over one of the most revered and sacred cathedrals in North America. The possibility of bringing a claim in this case wouldn't enter most people's minds.

But if the design of the steps was indeed flawed, why did the court dismiss Luz Montesinos's claim against St. Patrick's Cathedral without a trial? The court offered several reasons. First, the condition of the stairway was "open and obvious"—a circumstance that is arguably true of most stairs with unnecessarily risky designs. Second, the cathedral was exempt from New York City building code requirements because of its age.[8] But even without the benefit of a grandfather clause, the stairs would not have violated current code requirements because they were built on a slope. It was acceptable, given the uneven terrain, that the height of the first step above ground level varied from the left end of the stairway to the right. Third, St. Patrick's had provided a handrail in another location, and a conspicuous sign notified visitors that a handicap ramp was available at a different entrance. Fourth, the court found that St. Patrick's had notified the celebrants of World Marriage Day about the accessible entry options available to them. And finally—perhaps most revealing of attitudes toward this particular feature of New York City's physical environment—the court invoked "moral considerations arising from the view of society toward the relationship of the parties." In a "moral" contest with St. Patrick's Cathedral, a stubborn nonagenarian who refused assistance in climbing a staircase wouldn't stand a chance. Her decision to litigate in this case appears to defy all logic. The claim is ridiculous on its face.

CHAIRS

Although stairway falls rarely lead injury victims to attribute blame to anyone but themselves, the harm is immediately apparent. The victims know they've been hurt. They have no difficulty *naming* their injury, although few go on to *blame* someone else. But imagine a different kind of injury in which harm emerges more gradually over time. Consider, for example, the not-so-hypothetical case of a middle-aged office worker who suffers from back pain and spinal deformity. Unlike Luz Montesinos, this individual can't recall any traumatic incident that caused these symptoms, just the development of pain and disability over a period of years. In such circumstances, it's unlikely that she would even consider her pain and suffering to be an injury but merely part of the aging process. And if she did name her condition as an injury, she probably wouldn't blame another person for causing it. For this type of injury, moreover, *claiming* seems extraordinarily improbable—and even more ridiculous than filing a lawsuit after a fall on St. Patrick Cathedral's stairs. Lumping would nearly always be the expected response.

It may be surprising, then, to learn that back pain and spinal deformities can be caused by another familiar feature of our physical environment—the chair. We don't think much about chairs. Their presence in most environments doesn't appear to be the result of human choices among competing options or a preference for risky technologies over safer ones. Chairs are simply what we do with our bodies when we are not moving around or lying down. They seem almost like natural objects that belong in our homes, workplaces, and public areas, just as rocks and trees belong in parks and forests.

Yet Galen Cranz tells us there's nothing natural about chairs.[9] In some societies, people do not use chairs at all and simply squat, stand, or sit on the ground or floor. Where chairs do exist, their design varies greatly across cultures and social settings. Chairs are indeed the product of human design, and, according to Cranz, most chairs have one thing in common—they injure and sicken the people who use them.

Cranz recalls viewing a friend's photographs of men, women, and children living in Upper Volta. She noticed one individual who "stood beautifully, with wide shoulders that were neither pressed back under military tension nor rounded forward in a clerical stoop, and his chest was deep. His spine was erect and his head balanced, with no strain apparent in his neck muscles. I exclaimed at the perfection of his physical development." When she saw the photo of another man who also displayed perfect posture, she became curious about why these two individuals looked so different from others in the picture, as well as from the men and women she observed every day in America. The answer, it turned out, was quite simple: they "were the only two who had grown up in a village without a missionary school and its tables and chairs."[10] The chair is the culprit, according to Cranz. It compresses and deforms our spines, ruins our posture, and causes circulatory and digestive illnesses as well as serious pain.

Our culture has surely made too extensive a commitment to chairs to go back. We're unlikely to transform our physical environment so drastically as to eliminate chairs entirely and return to the healthier practice of sitting on the floor or standing up. But "sedentary scientists" tell us that we can improve things quite a lot by using stand-up desks and taking frequent breaks from sitting positions.[11] Moreover, there are better and worse designs for chairs. If the most advanced ergonomic practices were adopted, we could significantly reduce pain and suffering in our society. We could "minimize, but never completely eliminate, the damage caused by chair sitting."[12] The ideal chair would have lower seats, front rails that curve downward, seat depths and widths of only seventeen inches, less padding, and a space between the seat and the back of the chair. Adopting these changes in the design of most chairs would yield "an enormous benefit for public health."[13]

It seems, then, that the ailments of our hypothetical office worker could indeed be viewed as an injury. It was caused not only by making chairs a necessary component of the workplace but by designing them in a way that experts would consider dangerous to our health. Yet those who suffer the consequences of improper chair design are invisible in injury surveys. Their condition is likely be classified as an illness rather than the result of an accident. The naturalization of chairs as part of our physical environment tends to suppress both naming and blaming, and it makes claiming even more rare than in stairway accidents. Lumping of these injuries occurs as a matter of course, not as a conscious decision by the victim. Litigation is literally unthinkable.

The perception of chair-related illnesses and injuries as "natural" is likely to persist as long as chair-sitting for extended periods of time remains culturally normative. Scientists like James Levine are currently campaigning for a change in American perceptions about the health consequences of sitting, standing, working, and exercising;[14] and in the UK a movement called "Get Britain Standing" has been launched.[15] If such efforts succeed, a cognitive shift may occur and an enormous number of health problems in our society may either disappear or come to be viewed as injuries that could result in legal claims. Until that shift takes place, however, lumping will remain the only conceivable response to chair-related harms.

KEYBOARDS

The examples of stairs and chairs illustrate how our interactions with the physical environment can shape understanding of injuries in ways that increase lumping and decrease claiming. Countless other examples from the home and workplace lead to the same conclusion—our physical surroundings, and particularly our built environment, dramatically affect perceptions of injury. To cite just one more instance, it's widely known that cumulative trauma disorders (CTDs) are associated with long hours at the computer keyboard. Millions of Americans suffer this type of injury each year.[16] Yet it is not widely recognized that a significant cause of CTDs is the seemingly innocuous arrangement of the keys on the QWERTY keyboard.

The QWERTY keyboard, named after the left-to-right sequence of keys in the top row of letters, is not a "natural" layout, although it may seem so to those of us who learned to type at an early age. Rather, QWERTY is deliberately unnatural. It was first developed by Christopher Latham Sholes and Carlos S. Glidden for the Remington typewriter in the mid-nineteenth century. Their reason for adopting the QWERTY design is not entirely clear. As Sarah Lochlann Jain writes, "the usual explanation is that Sholes developed the layout to overcome typebar clash in early machines by placing the most frequently used type bars as far away from each other as possible."[17] If this is the case, the justification for the QWERTY design disappeared for most users when computers—which have no type bars— replaced typewriters. Yet, as Jain points out, the 1980s and 1990s brought a "vast increase in the use of the QWERTY keyboard" because of the ubiquity of the computer in the home as well as the workplace.[18]

The intentional awkwardness of the QWERTY layout puts

strain on the user for several reasons: (1) the left hand is over-worked in relation to the right hand; (2) certain fingers are overworked while others are underutilized; (3) the home row is underutilized in relation to the other rows; and (4) "fingers are required to execute an excessive amount of jumping back and forth from row to row."[19]

These shortcomings of the QWERTY keyboard, and its propensity to injure frequent users, have been well known since August Dvorak first published a highly critical study in 1943.[20] Dvorak and many others after him proposed alternate keyboard configurations, such as the split key design, that would alleviate muscle strain and reduce injuries. Yet the conventional QWERTY keyboard has persisted, causing highly preventable injuries to reach "epidemic" levels. Jain reports that, in 1989, 3.2 million repetitive stress injuries "were serious enough to take time away from jobs, adding up to 57 million lost workdays."[21] These figures do not include injuries caused by home use of computers. Moreover, Jain observes, current reporting practices may understate the number of workplace injuries by a factor of eight.

It's safe to say that most individuals who suffer keyboard-related injuries do not think to blame anyone. As Jain reports, a wave of lawsuits in the 1990s did allege, among other workstation problems, the harmfulness of the QWERTY design. These cases were, however, largely unsuccessful, and public perceptions didn't undergo a noticeable shift as a result. The effects of computer keyboard CTDs are not widely recognized, and those who suffer from them are likely to view their physical ailments as the inevitable encroachments of age and infirmity rather than as injuries. Even when keyboard users do *name* the injuries, they almost never *blame* the keyboard designers for using a layout that is known to cause harm rather than an alternate design that is safer. *Claiming* against keyboard manufacturers, at least since the litigation of the 1990s, is freakishly rare in comparison to the number of injuries. The reason is simple: the QWERTY keyboard is such a familiar part of our environment that we do not view it as an unnecessary risk that can hurt us. Instead, we view this particular human creation as natural, and we consider the safer alternatives to be odd and burdensome.

In sum, stairs, chairs, and keyboards have two things in common: they're associated with millions of injuries, and many times they are unnecessarily dangerous. Nonetheless, victims—and the general public—rarely connect these predictable injuries with risky designs. Instead, they blame the victims' carelessness, assumption of the risk, chance, or natural causes such as aging. Because people tend to accept certain features of the physical environment as "given," they ignore the human choices behind them. Preventable injuries come to seem natural, even to the victim, and the overwhelming predominance of lumping over claiming seems nothing more than common sense.

. . . AND AUTOMOBILES

Consumer products are a common feature of our physical environment, and the injuries they cause are among the most frequently litigated tort claims. Yet even with respect to product-related injuries, the ratio of lumping to claiming remains high. One explanation for the infrequency of product claims in relation to the injuries associated with them is the tendency to accept certain risky design features as inherent in the product rather than the result of a questionable decision by the manufacturer. What may actually be a flawed product design is widely viewed as a familiar—and natural—aspect of our normal physical environment. Only after an improved (and less risky) alternative design is introduced and accepted by the general public does the original dangerous defect come to seem obvious.

The automobile as a consumer product provides countless examples of the general tendency to naturalize risky design choices. Of course, automobiles carry with them certain inevitable risks, as one might expect of motorized vehicles the size of small rooms on wheels that hurtle down busy highways at high speeds, piloted in many instances by fallible drivers. Prudent design decisions could never completely eliminate auto-related accidents and injuries. Yet certain designs definitely make serious injuries more likely. For example, the Volkswagen Microbus, a popular vehicle in the 1960s, had no "crush space" in the front where a vehicle's engine is usually located. The distinctive design of the Microbus increased the chances that the driver, perched just inches from danger, would be injured in the event of a front-end collision. Should the producers of the Microbus have been held responsible for such injuries? The risk should have been immediately obvious to anyone who looked at the Microbus's box-like shape, yet it was considered natural and inevitable given the particular type of vehicle in question. When the issue was litigated, courts refused to hold that the Microbus had a design defect, even though Volkswagen could easily have prevented many deaths and injuries by replacing it with a vehicle of comparable size that had a protruding front hood with an engine inside.[22]

Similarly, at one time it appeared inevitable that automobile passengers in a violent collision could be thrown from the car or through the windshield. In the 1950s and 1960s, most people didn't think those injuries were caused by the automobile companies. The victims generally didn't lodge product liability claims based on faulty vehicle designs—they lumped them or blamed driver error instead. But today a car that lacks seatbelts and airbags to prevent "second impacts" is considered defective.[23] If a car without these safety features could somehow escape the federal regulatory net and reach consumers nowadays, injury claims against the manufacturers wouldn't seem outlandish at all. The absence of motor vehicle restraint systems no longer seems natural.

The physical environment is filled with products that could be made safer. There are many reasons why manufacturers place such products on the market without designing away the risk. In some instances, the risk—or the solution—is unknown. In other instances, the manufacturer's cost-benefit calculus does not support a safer but more expensive design, especially when relatively few potential injuries can be foreseen. In still other cases, "common sense" tells the manufacturer—and sometimes the consumer as well—that the risk is inherent in the product and it would be foolish to try to fix it. We don't put airbags on toboggans, though it might be technically possible to do so. The risks associated with some products seem natural, and safety measures seem awkward, bizarre, or intrusive. Until the safer design is widely accepted in the culture, consumers consider it perfectly normal to live with the risk. It appears to them to inhere in the product itself, and manufacturers generally prefer not to disturb that view. Lumping becomes the normal and expected outcome when injuries occur.

Views about "natural" risks in consumer products can change dramatically. A recent example is the rearview camera on passenger cars and vans. The new consensus that vehicles should come equipped with rearview cameras owes a great deal to the efforts of Dr. Greg Gulbransen, a Long Island pediatrician. Tragically, in October 2002, Dr. Gulbransen ran over and killed his two-year-old son, Cameron, while backing up in his own driveway. He later explained, "I never had a chance of seeing Cameron because he was too small. Too small for the large blind zones that are built into the design of our vehicles."[24] Gulbransen learned that Cameron was not the only victim of this kind of accident. According to recent estimates by federal regulators, 267 deaths and approximately 15,000 injuries are caused each year by vehicles backing up. The victims are mostly young children, in contrast to stair injuries, where the victims are mostly elderly.[25] One study found that 80 percent of individuals struck in driveways by cars backing up were, like Cameron Gulbransen, younger than five years old and the victims' average age was two years.[26]

For decades, Americans "naturalized" these accidents, and lumping rather than claiming was a foregone conclusion. The tragic deaths and injuries of very young children were considered inherent in the nature of motor vehicles. Cars are a ubiquitous feature of our physical environment, and they have certain unavoidable risks—including the driver's blind spot. Children should simply be kept away from driveways or streets where drivers can't see them when they shift into reverse.

The technology to reduce these tragic and rather frequent accidents has existed for some time. With a rearview camera and other simple devices, a significant number of injuries and fatalities could be prevented.[27] As many as half of the injuries, according to one experiment, could be eliminated if a sensor with an audible warning were combined with the camera.[28]

Dr. Gulbransen didn't agree that accidents like the one that killed his son were a natural concomitant of having automobiles. He campaigned to force automobile manufacturers to install better safety devices and, with the sponsorship of Senator Hillary Clinton and others, Congress eventually passed a bill that required NHTSA (National Highway Traffic Safety Administration) to enact rear visibility standards to reduce accidents caused by vehicles' blind spots. On February 28, 2008, President George W. Bush signed the Cameron Gulbransen Kids

Transportation Safety Act of 2007 into law. The road to implementation of the required safety standards was longer and bumpier than anticipated, but NHTSA finally published a rule in April 2014 requiring all new cars and light trucks to have rearview cameras by May 2018.[29]

In this instance, societal perspectives changed toward the risks that were normal and natural in automobiles. Many now believe that vehicles are defective and unsafe if they lack a rearview camera. By the 2013 model year, five years *before* the NHTSA mandate was to take effect, 53 percent of all new vehicles already offered cameras as standard equipment, and an additional 26 percent as optional.[30] This change occurred primarily because of a shift in the public's perception about the acceptable types and levels of risk that should be associated with a very familiar feature of our environment—the automobile. Injuries that were once viewed as inevitable or as the fault of the victims or their parents are now viewed as unnecessary and preventable. Before such a shift took place, however, lumping was the only response that made sense.

When Dr. Gulbransen refused to lump, he helped to launch a massive cultural shift. When shifts of this kind occur, more injuries are perceived as "actionable" that were previously seen as an unfortunate yet natural feature of our automotive age. Unless and until such a perceptual shift occurs, however, these injuries and others like them are almost certain to be lumped. Claiming seems nothing more than an inappropriate attempt to cash in on a child's misfortune and to shirk one's personal responsibility.

HOT COFFEE

Perhaps the most famous—and widely misunderstood—example of preventable product risk is the infamous McDonald's case, in which it was almost universally considered laughable for the victim to blame the restaurant after she spilled hot coffee on her own lap.[31] This was an injury most people thought Stella Liebeck should simply have lumped. One reason for the case's notoriety is that hot coffee is such a familiar feature of the physical environment. We see coffee and coffee cups every day. They're part of America's daily routine. We have deeply rooted assumptions about what risks are natural and unnatural when it comes to drinking hot coffee and how people should respond when they spill it.

Seventy-nine-year-old Stella Liebeck suffered third-degree burns on 6 percent of her body when she spilled the scalding cup of coffee while sitting in the passenger seat of a parked car.[32] After she successfully sued McDonald's for her injury, her case became an emblem of the tort reform movement, and she herself became a symbol of the litigious American out to make a fast buck from self-inflicted harm. Only later did it become apparent that Stella Liebeck was one of many victims of a deliberate and unusually risky design decision. Her injury resulted from a corporate policy to sell coffee at a temperature of 180–90 degrees, much hotter than other restaurants and far above the temperatures of 158–68 degrees of home-brewed coffee. McDonald's own experts admitted that anyone drinking coffee at such high temperatures would scald their throats.[33] It's not surprising that Stella Liebeck was described by her surgeon, Dr. Arredondo, as one of the worst burn cases from hot liquids that he had ever treated.

McDonald's had been put on notice by a number of similar accidents that their superheated coffee carried predictable risks of injury, yet they continued to expose their customers to the hazard until Liebeck's claim became widely publicized. Only then did they reduce the temperature of their coffee to more conventional levels and issue more conspicuous warnings on the cup. The idea of lodging a claim after spilling coffee on oneself seemed absurd, because the risk of harm was thought to be inherent in the product and obvious to all who bought it. Once McDonald's underlying decision about temperature levels was more carefully considered, however, it became evident that injuries like Stella Liebeck's were not "natural" but were the result of human choice. A known risk of serious harm could have been prevented by safer production practices.[34] Until design decisions of this kind are brought to light, lumping is the only response that makes sense to most people, and lodging a claim exposes injury victims such as Stella Liebeck to ridicule and public condemnation.

Sara Lachlann Jain contends that "unequally distributed physical injury"[35] associated with consumer products should not be viewed as accidental, but rather as a reflection of design decisions that encode deeper cultural understandings about whose lives and bodies should be protected or exposed to risk:

> Design decisions ineluctably code danger and injury at the outset of the production process. Products anticipate the agents that will animate them temporally and statistically; products and humans simulate imagined relationships and worlds. In this sense, Pintos and cheeseburgers are not so dissimilar, as they both demonstrate how American injury culture injures as a matter of course. . . . Elucidating the issues in this way raises the question of how human wounding counts, who "owns" health, and how it is to count as a social good.[36]

Although injuries appear to be "exceptional" events that randomly strike a few unlucky individuals, Jain argues that they are actually the consequence of "cultural work . . . which distributes goods and bads (such as risk, health, mobility, and injury) and also naturalizes cross-secting relations of subordination."[37]

CONCLUSION

Injuries take place within physical environments that imbue them with particular meanings, so that lodging a claim very often comes to appear selfish and ridiculous or even bizarre. Features of the physical environment can make claims seem inappropriate and can foster lumping in three different ways: (1) Some injuries are not even recognized *as injuries*. According to Galen Cranz, for example, chairs injure people, but the harms they cause are commonly viewed as illness or the effects of aging, and they are seldom connected to the use of chairs. (2) People may suffer injuries without realizing they result from conscious choices made by others. When a product manufacturer has selected a particular level of risk, that decision may not be known by the victim. Without realizing that safer choices are possible—such as rearview cameras to guard against injuries to children in the family driveway—the victim thinks of the accident as natural and unavoidable. (3) Injury victims and the general public may blame those who are harmed for their failure to avoid the mishap. Elderly people who fall on stairs or spill scalding coffee in their laps are deemed totally responsible for their own injuries, even though the stair designer or the coffee seller could have anticipated and reduced the risk.

Injury victims' perspectives on these and other injuries result from the ways in which they interact with their physical environment—with the spaces through which they move, the objects they encounter, and the meanings with which their culture imbues those objects. Very often the nature of these interactions leads victims to the conclusion that lumping is far more appropriate than claiming. This perception can be changed, as the cases of automobile airbags and rearview cameras illustrate. But until the victims' basic views and assumptions are transformed and the underlying choices exposed, many injuries are naturalized. Lumping is the norm. Indeed, it appears to the victims and those around them to be the only sensible response, and claiming remains extremely rare.

EIGHT

THE SOCIAL AND CULTURAL
ENVIRONMENT OF INJURIES

In 2005, the late novelist David Foster Wallace
delivered a commencement address at Kenyon
College that began with the following story:

> There are these two young fish swimming
> along and they happen to meet an older fish
> swimming the other way, who nods at them
> and says, "Morning, boys, how's the water?"
>
> And the two young fish swim on for a bit,
> and then eventually one of them looks over at
> the other and goes, "What the hell is water?"[1]

It's often said that culture is like the water in
which fish swim. We seldom give it much thought,
but it surrounds us and shapes our every idea
and action. The social and cultural environment
constantly affects our perceptions and behavior,
although it's far less visible than the physical environment discussed in chapter 7. Wallace's fish
don't even know what water is. Americans are often just as oblivious, and we may think it's only
other people who have culture. What we do is just
"normal."

Culture makes the social world seem natural
or inevitable, even though it's actually contingent

and varies enormously across time and space. Unlike fish's aquatic environment, however, culture is a human creation. As Clifford Geertz famously observed, humans fabricate culture just as spiders fabricate their webs, and then they find themselves suspended in their own creation.[2] The ideas, images, practices, and institutions that people develop over time don't even feel human-made. They become part of the "of course" nature of everyday life. They seem beyond question.

As this book continues to explore the roots of lumping in injury cases, it's essential to consider how the ideas and perceptions of injury victims emerge from the organic connection of mind and culture. The previous chapter applied the model developed in chapter 5 and discovered that lumping results in part from how humans interact with their physical environment. People's perception of stairs, chairs, automobiles, and the other objects they encounter in their daily lives can determine how they respond to the pain such encounters may cause. In this chapter, as we continue to search for a solution to the mystery of the missing plaintiff, our focus on the environment of injuries expands from the physical to the social and cultural contexts in which injuries arise (acknowledging, of course, that there's no bright line separating the two). Some of our most important clues about lumping await discovery in this phase of the investigation.

LUMPING BY THOSE WHO DON'T THINK THEY WERE INJURED

When is an injury not an injury? Individuals who don't think they've suffered an injury wouldn't normally lodge a claim—lumping would be the only sensible response. It's possible that much of the lumping that goes on in our society is associated with *noninjuries*, that is, painful or harmful experiences that are somehow not interpreted as injurious. Without *naming*, there can be no *claiming*. But under what circumstances might individuals differ in their perception that an injury has occurred? To answer this question, we must first recognize that injuries are not objective facts. Injuries are not things in the world. They're events that humans in specific social environments habitually name as harmful. What is construed as an injury in one cultural setting may be considered nonharmful or even beneficial in another. The very concept of an injury reflects a deep interaction between humans and their social and cultural environment.

The dictionary defines injury as "an act that damages or hurts."[3] Wouldn't everyone at least agree about what hurts—about the presence or absence of pain? Not necessarily. It turns out that pain itself is not a universal constant. Pain, like injury, is a cultural construct that results in variable perceptions. As Mary Moore Free observes, "while the stimulation of pain fibers to tell the brain that something is wrong is the same among all human beings, the perceptions and control of pain vary from society to society."[4]

Although nearly all humans are susceptible to pain, differences in the cultural environment can shape the cognition of painful events in quite different ways. Jean E. Jackson states, "As with bodies in general, the painful body simultaneously produces and is produced by culture, reflecting and reproducing it." Jackson goes on to note that the experience of pain does not simply involve a pain receptor registering the unpleasant stimulus and sending the bad news to the brain. Rather, anthropologists and cognitive scientists now understand that pain is perceived through complex and multidirectional exchanges involving the body, mind, and social environment. She refers to these as "two-way flows along multiple pathways involving cognitive, emotional, and behavioral inputs," which together produce a signal of pain.[5] Our sense of pain emerges from the interaction of body, mind, and cultural environment.

Some American soldiers in World War II required less than usual amounts of pain medication for their injuries because they positively associated their wounds with a "ticket home with honor."[6] Broken bones and lacerations may seem extremely painful and debilitating to an office worker or a classroom teacher but less so to a farmer[7] or a rugby player,[8] for whom they are a normal and expected hazard of everyday activities. The painfulness and severity of an injury is, of course, directly relevant to claiming behavior by the victim. In social or cultural contexts in which an injury is viewed as less severe, or even as beneficial, pursuit of a claim is much less likely.[9] Physical hazing of a football recruit has often been interpreted as a desirable way to prepare him for the rigors of the sport rather than as the infliction of pain. Such conduct *shouldn't hurt* if the athlete is tough enough and ready for full-on contact. It seldom leads to a claim for compensation, even when it leaves permanent physical or emotional scars.

If pain can vary from one cultural context to another, so does the cultural construction of injury itself. In one setting, a painful experience may not be perceived as an injury, while in another it could be viewed in a very different light. Consider, for example, the now obsolete practice of foot binding in China. Without question, foot binding imposed pain and permanent bodily disfiguration on young girls. Here's how Jung Chang describes her grandmother's experience at the age of two:

> [My grandmother's] mother, who herself had bound feet, first wound a piece of white cloth about twenty feet long round her feet, bending all the toes except the big toe inward and under the sole. Then she placed a large stone

on top to crush the arch. My grandmother screamed in agony and begged her to stop. Her mother had to stick a cloth into her mouth to gag her. My grandmother passed out repeatedly from the pain.

The little girl's suffering did not end with this initial agonizing episode. Her feet had to remain bound at all times to prevent them from healing and returning to normal shape. As Chang notes, "For years my grandmother lived in relentless, excruciating pain." But her mother told her that she must endure this agony to ensure "her own future happiness." Normal feet would "bring shame on the husband's household." Bound feet were considered beautiful, erotic, and supremely significant among the privileged classes.[10]

Clearly, these young girls experienced horrible pain. But did they suffer an injury as a result? From the perspective of contemporary American society, the answer is obviously yes. If someone were to practice foot binding today, we would be appalled. We would certainly see it as profoundly injurious, because the practice causes pain, suffering, and lifelong mobility impairment. During one period in Chinese history, however, and within a particular sector of Chinese society, bound feet were not considered an injury. They were viewed, by some at least, as a mark of beauty and nobility. As long as servants were available to carry high-ranking women from place to place, the inability to walk was not disabling, although it would become so in any other social setting.[11] In this particular social and cultural context, foot binding was simply not seen as injurious.

Perhaps the practice of foot binding is too exotic to be relevant to issues of lumping and claiming in American society today. If so, there are other examples closer to home—such as the circumcision of male infants. Like foot binding, male circumcision can be viewed in two very different ways. Many people see it as a routine health measure and even a sacred practice. Others insist that it is a cruel and painful injury inflicted on a helpless child.

Male circumcision was among the three most common surgeries in the United States in 2005.[12] In that year, more than 1.2 million circumcisions were performed on 56 percent of newborn male babies. The practice of male circumcision has roots in both religious belief and modern medical science, although it has recently become controversial. As Sarah E. Waldeck explains, American medicine routinized male circumcision in the late nineteenth century, when surgical removal of the male infant's foreskin was thought to prevent a broad spectrum of diseases and deformities.[13] Circumcision remained a medically endorsed practice until the American Academy of Pediatrics first recommended against its routine use in 1971.[14] Subsequently, the AAP changed its position to one of neutrality in 1989 and again to disapproval in 1999. With each of these policy shifts, the rate of circumcision rose and fell. By 2009, it had dropped to 32.5 percent of male newborns, with substantial variation across different regions of the United States.[15]

The practice of male circumcision has roots extending far back into human history. As Michael J. Weila explains,

In Judaism, the obligation of male circumcision is found in Genesis (the first book of the Pentateuch). The biblical text teaches that God appeared to Abraham at age ninety-nine to "establish My covenant between Me and you." Under the covenant, God promised Abraham and his offspring all the land of Canaan (biblical Israel). In exchange for God's promise, the Jewish people were instructed to "circumcise the flesh of your foreskin." . . . Genesis mandates that uncircumcised men be cast out of the community.[16]

Ritual circumcision among Jews, performed by an officiant known as a mohel, takes place on the eighth day after birth. In Islam, too, male circumcision has for centuries been viewed as a key element of the faith, sometimes performed in early infancy and sometimes later in life.

Evidence indicates that this widespread and, for some, sacred practice actually is painful. One might think that a newborn wouldn't feel much pain, but recent studies suggest otherwise. As Waldeck observes,

> Circumcision is painful enough that when it is performed after infancy, general anesthesia is the standard of care. In part, this is because no local anesthetic can completely block the pain of circumcision. In addition, the most effective local anesthesia involves multiple injections into the penis, which are thought to be too painful for the fully-aware patient to tolerate. . . . Yet most of us are remarkably cavalier about the prospect of infants experiencing the pain of circumcision. One common misperception is that infants are not yet sufficiently developed to feel pain. But newborns have both the anatomical and functional components necessary for the perception of painful stimuli.[17]

If circumcision really is painful, then should it be viewed as the deliberate infliction of an injury on a subject incapable of consenting—or resisting? A devout Jew or Muslim would certainly object to this characterization and wouldn't view circumcision as an injury in any sense of the word. Dena S. Davis quotes one mohel's response to the critique of circumcision:

> There is a misconception that pain is a bad thing to be avoided at all cost. Pain is part of life as a human being. We could not survive without pain. . . . We could not grow and

learn as individuals without pain. You cannot give your child a life without pain. The consequence of doing that would be disastrous.

The question to be asked is not is there any pain, but is the pain tolerable? Regarding infant circumcision without anesthesia the answer is certainly yes. . . . All babies undergoing circumcision have undergone a much more prolonged and painful experience than circumcision. That experience is not elective, we don't choose to be born, but we are.[18]

Yet criticism of male circumcision is growing. Some view it not as a joyous rite conferring membership into a community of the faithful, or as a beneficial health precaution, but as a cruel and painful mutilation forced on a powerless subject. From their perspective, male circumcision is not only a tort but also a form of child abuse. William E. Brigman, for example, has written, "cultural astigmatism . . . prevents contemporary Americans from perceiving or acknowledging the most widespread form of child abuse in society today: child mutilation through routine neonatal circumcision of males."[19]

This critical view of male circumcision as an injury and a human rights violation has achieved traction in a few societies around the world. Courts and legislatures in some countries, including South Africa and Sweden, have imposed restrictions on circumcisions performed in nonmedical settings[20] and have even attempted to criminalize the practice (in May 2012, a German appellate court declared the practice illegal but was overturned legislatively two months later).[21]

It's difficult to say whether the convergence of medical doubts about male circumcision and claims of human rights violations will lead to a growing public perception of this practice as a form of injury. It seems unlikely that such a position will ever gain widespread acceptance within Jewish and Muslim communities, where male circumcision remains central to an entire belief system. The tension between the injury versus noninjury viewpoints does, however, provide a fascinating example of the cultural contingency of the concept of injury itself. According to Marie Fox and Michael Thomson, the cultural framing of male circumcision is not just religious. It also reflects basic understandings of male and female identity. In their view,

> circumcision has functioned as a marker of masculine belonging. By literally inscribing particular identity/ies on the infant male body, circumcision can be understood as a normalising technology which validates particular forms of body modification; in this case the removal of tissue which comes to be coded as excessive, redundant, polluted or feminine.[22]

Thus, we should not view the injury/noninjury issue as distinctively religious. Just as some people in China didn't consider foot binding injurious because of cultural ideals of feminine beauty, so might other practices, including circumcision, seem noninjurious because of cultural ideals of masculinity.

The broader point, for purposes of this chapter, is that cultural images and ideologies can determine what kinds of painful experiences come to be defined as injuries. Only after passing this definitional threshold, only after *naming* the harm, can the possibility of a claim become thinkable. A few tort claims of circumcision as injury have begun to appear in American courts, brought by one of the parents or other legal representatives, but none to date has been successful.[23] Unless public perceptions change in our society, millions of circumcision "victims" will simply accept the pain and move on; and claiming will remain infrequent and futile. The case of male circumcision vividly illustrates how the social and cultural environment can foster lumping for enormous numbers of painful experiences.

LUMPING BY THOSE WHO CONSIDER IT WRONG TO CLAIM

Even among individuals who perceive themselves to have been injured, many choose to lump rather than claim because of images and values that prevail in the social and cultural environment. Culture imbues the options available to a self-perceived injury victim with very specific meanings. For example, sticking up for one's rights can be seen as admirable in one cultural context but as selfish and destructive in another. Conversely, enduring one's pain without any response at all can be viewed as virtuous, stoic, and even "manly" in one cultural setting but as cowardly or insensitive to social justice concerns in another. It makes sense that injury victims would tend to prefer lumping over claiming in cultural contexts that exalt self-reliance and individual responsibility over the assertion of material interests.

Lawrence M. Friedman has written eloquently and extensively about popular legal culture, which he defines as "people's ideas, attitudes, and expectations about law and legal process."[24] Popular legal culture is like the water in which fish swim; it shapes people's response to injuries even when they aren't aware of it. Friedman asserts that modern American legal culture is characterized by an expectation that injuries should be compensated: "There has developed in this country what I call here a *general expectation of justice,* and a *general expectation of recompense for injuries and loss.* Together, these make up a demand for . . . 'total justice.'"[25]

Friedman contends that the norm of total justice is associated with a "law explosion" in American society. By this he means that law, legal rights, and the expectation of compensation are expanding to areas of life that formerly weren't viewed in legal terms. A shift in American legal culture during the second half of the twentieth century encouraged people to perceive their experiences—including their injuries—in terms of rights violations and potential legal claims. Friedman is careful not to equate this shift to an increase in the absolute number of legal claims, which, he notes, would be difficult to quantify. Nevertheless, in his view, "total justice" expectations have become pervasive in our society, leading to a backlash among those who oppose the perceived law explosion.

Although Friedman marshals impressive support for his hypothesis about American legal culture, there is considerable counterevidence tending to contradict the view that our society has become more legalized at the neighborhood or community levels. In fact, some who have studied American popular culture in the late twentieth and early twenty-first centuries have concluded that it tends to be far more supportive of lumping than claiming. Less than a decade after Friedman published *Total Justice*, Carol Greenhouse, Barbara Yngvesson, and I wrote a book drawing on ethnographic studies of American law and culture in three communities in New England, the Southeast, and the Midwest.[26] In these settings, we found a widespread condemnation of litigation and claiming. Longtime residents viewed the aggressive assertion of injury claims as antisocial and "uncultured," and they associated such claims with people whom they deemed outsiders to the community. In fact, claiming behavior was an important marker of social marginality. Those who considered themselves insiders believed that anyone who accepted the local culture would prefer to lump injuries rather than pursue compensation, and they denounced those who did otherwise:

[Lumping] emerges as a culturally appropriate means of resolving some of the contradictions between self-interest and the collective good. Its counterpart, confrontation, which is derived from conceptions of individualism based on rights and entitlements and is associated with the stereotype of the outsider, utterly fails this test. Confrontation, viewed from this perspective, appears to pit the individual irreconcilably against the collectivity. From the same perspective, whatever gains an individual may obtain by invoking law are at the expense of the community.[27]

Cultural norms opposed to claiming were not mere abstractions. They shaped people's behavior and marked community boundaries in very powerful ways. For example, one woman in the pseudonymous community of Sander County, Illinois, told me of the choice she had to make after her daughter was killed by a negligent driver. She and her husband wanted to sue the man who was responsible, but they decided that, if they planned to remain in Sander County, they would have to accept a relatively small insurance settlement and lump the rest. In her words,

One of the reasons that I was extremely hesitant to sue was because of the community pressure. . . . Local people in this community are not impressed when you tell them that you're involved in a lawsuit. . . . That really turns them off. . . . They're not impressed with people who don't earn their own way. And that's taking money that they're not sure that you deserve.[28]

Similarly, a Sander County farmer told me that his wife had suffered a serious and permanent injury when she fell down the stairs at a neighbor's house. Although he considered the neighbor negligent, he and his wife simply lumped the injury and never made a claim of any kind. His story was typical. The local culture encouraged self-sufficiency and viewed claiming as greedy and socially destructive. When it came to personal injuries in these three communities, the expectation was not "total justice" but law avoidance. It's possible that the legal culture in large urban areas would strike a different balance in favor of claiming rather than lumping, but there is no persuasive evidence that this is the case. As we have seen from the national surveys discussed in chapter 2, the vast majority of injuries in America result in lumping. It's unlikely this would be true if the behavior of urban residents actually tended to reflect an expectation *and pursuit* of total justice in personal injury cases.

In short, even though the language of rights and legal recourse is widely used in America, the social and cultural surroundings of injury victims do not necessarily encourage claiming. The very opposite appears to be the case in many settings, where lumping is the expected response when an upright citizen suffers injury. Claiming is considered selfish and socially destructive. Injury victims who demand recompense run the very real risk of becoming social outcasts in their own communities.

FACTORS SHAPING A CULTURE OF LUMPING

If culture is indeed a human creation, unlike the streams, lakes, and oceans in which fish swim, why has it taken this distinctive form? Why has lumping become the preferred response to personal injuries in America, and what is the source of the powerful currents that discourage and even stigmatize claiming?

As we saw in chapter 6, repeat player "haves" can exert a disproportionate influence on the shape of tort law, and it's in their interest to limit the liability of injurers. Injury victims are predominantly people with lower social status and fewer resources. Those who cause injuries are usually persons or corporations with deeper pockets.[29] It's not surprising that, on the whole, the haves in our society tend to oppose claiming and seek to limit the role of tort law in society.

The influence exerted by haves is not confined to the shaping of legal doctrine but extends to the shaping of culture itself. Since haves tend to view matters from a defendant's perspective, they are likely to endorse the philosophy of "personal responsibility" and self-sufficiency and to condemn claiming and litigation. Injuries, from this perspective, very often appear inevitable, nobody's fault, or the result of the injury victim's own carelessness. These views are more likely to shape popular culture than the contrary perspective of injuries as rights violations or as threats to the well-being of society—a perspective that is generally associated with plaintiffs in injury cases. So powerful are the effects of norms generated by the haves that it is not uncommon for have-nots to adopt them, even in contradiction to their own interests. Paradoxically, persons of lower socioeconomic status who are most likely to benefit from personal injury claims very often espouse an anticlaiming perspective, simply because they have internalized the predominant cultural norms favoring lumping.

How exactly do these anticlaiming perspectives achieve predominance in the social and cultural environment? One way is through the media. William Haltom and Michael McCann's book, *Distorting the Law*, shows how anticlaiming supporters influence the media to disseminate ideas and images that support lumping.[30] This perspective is, in their study, closely aligned with the agenda of the tort reform movement. Haltom and McCann surveyed the content of thousands of newspaper articles and editorials dealing with tort law issues and found that the mass media tended to communicate the ideology of "individual responsibility" rather than the equally legitimate ideology of risk reduction and corporate responsibility. Individual responsibility has become a catchphrase for those who oppose claiming and litigation by injury victims.

Why should the media, even in news articles that appear neutral, tend to view tort issues most often through this anticlaiming lens? The authors persuasively show that the dominant media perspective grew directly from a strategy coordinated by the Manhattan Institute, the American Tort Reform Association (ATRA), APCO, and locally based Citizens against Lawsuit Abuse (CALA) organizations, with funding from insurance companies, large corporations, and "wealthy individual patrons and foundations that traditionally have supported conservative, pro-business causes, including the John Olin Foundation, the Sarah Scaife Foundation, and the Starr Foundation."[31] A massive advertising campaign in the 1980s and 1990s disseminated the anticlaiming viewpoint in clear and simple terms, offering unsupported claims about a supposed explosion of personal injury litigation and its detrimental effects on American business and on insurance premiums.

At the same time, voices on the other side of the policy debate were weak or ineffectual in their impact on popular culture. Referring to the proplaintiff American Trial Lawyers Association, Haltom and McCann title one of their chapters, "ATLA Shrugged." Tort reformers have been far more savvy in their media strategies than those who speak for injury victims. The mass media came to be dominated by ideas and images associated with a highly critical and politically conservative view of personal injury claimants, and the contrary view became relatively invisible. The tort reform campaign, as we saw in chapter 1, was extraordinarily successful in shaping public opinion about injuries and claiming. It produced a cultural shift.

Norms opposing injury claims expanded outward from news reporting to other venues of cultural production. Wittingly or not, reporters, cartoonists, editorial writers, and even late night talk show hosts adopted the tort reform perspective. The McDonald's hot coffee case, whose facts and outcome were distorted beyond recognition by inept reporting, achieved iconic status in American culture. It seemed to symbolize everything that was wrong with our supposedly litigious culture. Surely seventy-nine-year-old Stella Liebeck, who carelessly spilled coffee on her own lap, supposedly while driving a car, should have taken responsibility for her injury and lumped her claim rather than seeking millions of dollars from the family-friendly McDonald's corporation. Never mind that Ms. Liebeck was not actually the driver of the car, that it was parked at the time of the accident, that she had originally sought only her medical expenses, that she eventually settled for less than $480,000, that McDonald's was on notice that their superheated coffee exceeded industry standards and had injured other consumers before her, that her third-degree burns were extremely serious, and that an initially skeptical jury became outraged over what they saw as McDonald's callous indifference.[32] The true facts of the case became irrelevant in the rush to denounce the elderly injury victim for shamelessly bringing a claim at all.

The mass media do not operate alone to influence our cultural perspective on claiming versus lumping, but they are an important factor. They show us clearly how wealth, power, and political ideology can shape culture and create a set of ideas and images that affect popular perspectives on injuries. Cultural frameworks of this kind influence people's thought processes even when they don't realize it, including the decisions of those who are injured. Injury victims come to share the predominant "personal responsibility" perspective, and they choose their response accordingly.

Furthermore, the law itself can contribute to the shaping of these cultural attitudes. Law and society are mutually constitutive. Law can—at least under some circumstances—powerfully influence the social and cultural environment at the same time that the environment shapes the law. For example, the caps on pain and suffering adopted in many American states are undoubtedly the product of widespread anticlaiming norms in the social and cultural environment.[33] They illustrate how the social environment can shape the law. But, conversely, these laws—the legislation capping damage awards—affect the social and cultural environment by communicating the message that claims for pain and suffering are problematic and relatively unimportant.[34] In a more general sense, the creation of such caps reinforces the message that personal injury claimants, unless they are restrained by the law, will simply run amok. They will seek every opportunity to take advantage of hapless defendants. This negative message, heard often enough, can filter back to the perceptions and interpretations that arise nonconsciously from the moment an injury is experienced. In other words, caps on damage awards are both a product of and contributor to the process of cultural production.

Cultural perspectives in our social surroundings are not monolithic. In a society as large, pluralistic, differentiated, and stratified as ours, we would expect to find varied perspectives on most issues, and that includes personal injuries. It is surely true that many injury victims are influenced by a desire for "total justice" and that some are quick to assert a claim even in trivial or nonmeritorious cases. Yet there is substantial evidence that a contrary perspective has become far more dominant in the current social and cultural environment. Public discourse and the media are saturated with anticlaiming perspectives, the rate of lumping vastly exceeds the rate of claiming in injury cases, and tort litigation remains rare and has steadily declined in recent decades. The factors shaping our legal culture strongly reinforce lumping, and they disvalue and discourage claiming.

LUMPING BY THOSE WHO FEAR
THE CONSEQUENCES OF CLAIMING

As we've seen, the cultural environment can influence the thoughts and decisions of injury victims in subtle but powerful ways. Victims may reach decisions or abstain from thinking and acting in response to an injury without even realizing that their ideas were shaped from beginning to end by the surrounding culture. But in other instances, lumping occurs because of less subtle pressures. There are many cases in which the injury victim does indeed want to assert a claim but must settle for lumping out of fear or intimidation.

Socially marginalized or disempowered people who fear personal consequences may feel they have no choice but to suffer an injustice and give up any thought of claiming. Individuals who are injured in the workplace, for example, often conclude that lumping is safer than complaining, because they don't want to place their job or career prospects in jeopardy. These concerns may become particularly acute when the victims fear biased reactions based on their gender, race, cultural difference, or sexual orientation.[35] Rape in the workplace is a form of personal injury known to result in lumping precisely because of these concerns, as well as the often-justified fear that the victim will not be believed and will be viewed as a liar and troublemaker.[36]

Similar considerations may prevail when injuries occur in other social settings. In Sander County, a Latina woman whose husband was injured in a local tavern expressed her opposition to his pursuit of a legal remedy in the following terms: "I was afraid that maybe they'd say our kind of people are just trying to get their hands on money any way we could."[37] In cases such as these, inequalities or discrimination in the social environment can affect perceptions and decision making and can lead injury victims to lump claims even when they wish very much to demand justice.

CONCLUSION

Injuries and injury responses occur in specific social and cultural environments where values and worldviews are widely shared. Perhaps it's a mistake to speak too broadly about American culture or Japanese, Italian, or Australian cultures. Within the boundaries of an entire nation-state, there are many kinds of communities and many forms of "local knowledge" associated with distinctive cultural norms and values.[38] Nevertheless, in contemporary mass societies, powerful forces cut across all communities and produce far-reaching images and understandings of injury. Two of these forces are the media and the law.

The social and cultural environment plays a critically important role in the process of cognition and decision making that follows an injury. Indeed, the environment shapes the very perception that an injury has or has not occurred, as well as the appropriate range of responses by the victim. As we have seen in earlier chapters of this book, the self and the environment are not distinct entities but are organically linked. The environmental factors we have discussed in this chapter are not outside the self, but actually constitute it. They become active even in the nonconscious cognition that is crucial to the interpretation of harmful experiences.

This view of the self and its environment does not alone explain why lumping predominates over claiming among injury victims. It does, however, provide powerful evidence for our investigation of the dog that doesn't bark. The discussion in this chapter points to a number of environmental factors that could lead an injured person to absorb harm while remaining silent and taking no action against the injurer. These include the naturalization of injury and the emergence of value systems that encourage self-sufficiency or stoicism rather than the demand for a remedy. And, even when injury victims might wish they could assert a claim, they may hesitate because they fear stigma or overt reprisal. The pervasiveness of such values reflects disparities in social and political power and the unequal capacity to create and disseminate influential social norms. All of these social and cultural factors promote lumping over claiming.

The widespread tendency to lump personal injuries should, after all, come as no surprise. We live in a social and cultural environment where claiming is very often seen as a significant threat not just to the economy but to the moral fiber of our nation. Rather than viewing injury claims as an essential means for deterring risky behavior and making victims whole, we have come to view claimants themselves—and their lawyers—as socially destructive parasites who must be restrained for the good of us all.

NINE

THE INFLUENCE OF OTHERS
AND THE DECISION TO LUMP

||||||||||||||||||||||||||||||||||||||||||||||||||||||||||||||||||||||||||||||||||||||||||||||||||||||||||||||||||||||||

As we make our way through life, are we basically solitary figures who encounter new experiences alone and respond to them without consulting or considering the views of other people? Do we carry a bundle of rights on our back and decide in isolation whether or not to use them? The very idea of humans as completely autonomous and independent creatures seems unsettling and almost surreal. We are inherently social beings. Our experiences, perceptions, and judgments occur within a network of relationships connecting us with others, who affect our thoughts and actions in crucially important ways. These social connections must be considered in the quest to understand why injury victims lump rather than claim. In this chapter, we turn to a final feature of the model of injury perception and response presented in chapter 5—the influence of others.

The importance of social relationships for understanding cognition and legal behavior is now widely recognized. As we shall see, social scientists reject the idea of the autonomous self and have proposed creative ways to explore how perceptions, judgments, and decisions emerge from our social relationships. Even the most rugged individualist can't think or act in a vacuum. Her ideas are shaped by her interactions with other people and by their expectations, values, and preferences. The model from figure 5.3 requires us to examine how these interpersonal connections occur and why they lead injury victims to reject the possibility of bringing a claim against the injurer—or never even to consider it.

Furthermore, if we view the injury victim in terms of her relationships with others, the very concept of an injury begins to transform itself. The harm inflicted on the victim is actually a harm to others as well, since their lives, emotions, and resources may also be affected. Our ideas about injuries may be too narrow, too restricted by an ideology of sturdy individualism. In real life, when serious injuries take place, there's almost no such thing as an individual victim. Harms are nearly always collective.

The myth of the autonomous self remains strong in our society, mostly because of our tradition of personal independence and individual rights. Discussions of tort law tend to focus on harm to individuals and not groups. But there are exceptions. Martha Chamallas and Jennifer B. Wriggins, for example, have emphasized the importance for tort law of "relational harms," such as the emotional trauma parents suffer when they witness a negligent act causing the death or serious injury of their child.[1] And other feminist legal scholars have argued persuasively for recognition of what Jennifer Nedelsky calls "the relational self" since, she observes, "each individual is in basic ways constituted by networks of relationships of which they are a part."[2] Further, Martha Fineman emphasizes that everyone is vulnerable to "harm, injury, and misfortune." Consequently, we are all potentially dependent on our particular web of relationships, both personal and institutional, and that's where we look for support if misfortune strikes.[3] None of us is truly independent and autonomous. A serious injury always has an impact on the victim's social network and not on the victim alone.

The model of perception and response presented in chapter 5 requires us to add this final element to our investigation. We turn now to a consideration of the various ways in which the victim's relationships and social interactions help to explain why lumping is so common in our society and claiming so rare.

THE INFLUENCE OF OTHERS: A CASE STUDY

We begin with a story from Sander County, Illinois, where I conducted research more than thirty years ago. The story vividly illustrates how an injury victim—in this case the mother of a seriously injured child—formulated her views of the accident under the influence of her former husband and then reformulated them in an entirely different way under the influence of her pastor. In both cases, her relationship with others had a profound importance for her decision to make a claim and her ultimate rejection of that decision in favor of lumping.

It was no coincidence that Reverend Charlton Fillmore, a recent arrival in Sander County and a blue-collar worker, ministered to the community's newcomers—the outsiders and the underclass.[4] Most of his congregation worked in local factories or were unemployed. Reverend Fillmore himself was the custodian at a local school. He and other members of the Salvation Assembly Church knew the pain of divorce, economic hardship, and uprootedness.

In an interview, Reverend Fillmore observed that the lifelong residents of Sander County lived very different lives from those of his parishioners. Those with local roots were "much more stable than people that come and go and are always moving around." They had more "contentment." When problems arose, the well-established farming families and longtime small business owners reacted "more sensibly and more conservatively."

By contrast, Reverend Fillmore's parishioners were "always looking for something different or somewhere different to find a happier life. . . . They're looking for more money. They're searching for something." The idyllic farming community of Sander County, with its attractive houses and scenic pastures, was not their world. They lived in pain, disorder, and impermanence. "I believe there are a lot of hurting people . . . that have been scarred for various, because of various backgrounds, searching, somebody searching for purpose. . . . There's a lot more hurt that goes on than what we realize."

Miranda Compton, one of the newcomers to Sander County, had converted to born-again Christianity and joined the Salvation Assembly Church by the time I interviewed her. Reverend Fillmore's description of his parishioners fit her perfectly. Before her religious rebirth, she had faced troubles that all but crushed her spirit. Her husband had physically abused her, and she divorced him, only to marry him a second time several years later, after she had set her spiritual affairs in order.

During her brief experience as a single parent, Miranda had felt humiliated by accepting welfare checks. She thought she had strayed in other ways as well. She smoked and drank, and she found her four children difficult to manage and injury prone. Her youngest child, Lily, had suffered a particularly serious injury, which eventually became the subject of one of the rare tort cases filed in the Sander County court.[5] In retrospect, Miranda regarded her decision to consult a lawyer and file a lawsuit as one of the worst of her life. She attributes the decision primarily to the influence of her then-ex-husband.

The accident occurred in August, just a few days before the start of school. Lily, a five-year-old, was playing unsupervised in the alley behind their apartment, when she saw a large dumpster belonging to a local automobile dealership. The dumpster had a protruding handle that looked to Lily like a monkey bar, and she began to swing on it upside down. There was no warning sign, and the dumpster was positioned on a small hill. Unbalanced by her swinging, the dumpster tipped over and fell on her. It was very heavy, so heavy that Miranda's ex-husband couldn't lift it when he later went back to the scene of the accident. But as Lily lay pinned beneath the dumpster, screaming in pain, her thirteen-year-old sister somehow found the strength to free her and carry her away. Both girls were soaked with Lily's blood.

Lily was hospitalized for a week as the doctors struggled to stop her internal bleeding. Miranda worried that Lily's condition could "develop into something more serious in later years" and might affect her ability to have children. Still, Miranda was not inclined to pursue any claim against the trash removal company that owned the dumpster or the automobile dealership that left it unguarded as an attractive nuisance for local children. All her current medical costs were covered by insurance, but, as Lily grew older, additional expenses might arise that would be impossible to handle. Miranda worried about future financial burdens for herself and for Lily.

Despite these concerns, Miranda would have lumped Lily's injury had her ex-husband not persuaded her to see a lawyer and lodge a claim: "I really didn't want to sue, but my husband, he said that I should. . . . He prompted me into going to see a lawyer about it and so I, well, I finally did." Miranda was disgusted with the legal process, although the case never went to trial. She believed that lawyers don't really represent their clients' interests but simply "go into a room and they're pretending that they're in there battling for you and then the whole time they're negotiating together." The attitude of the lawyers seemed to be "the longer we draw this thing out, the more money you and I are going to make." Although the lawsuit originally claimed damages in the amount of $150,000, her lawyer settled the case for $3,000, of which he retained $1,000 as his fee. In the end, Miranda received only $2,000 to cover any future medical complications.

Miranda's decision to claim rather than lump Lily's injury resulted from the influence of a third party. It was not the choice she would have made by herself, but her ex-husband was still a strong presence in her life, and she accepted his view about how one should respond to a potentially serious harm. It's possible, of course, that her husband's history of physical abuse made it easier for him to impose his will on Miranda.

Miranda's story illustrates the importance of relationships in the decision-making process. But Miranda's narrative also reflects another powerful influence on her thinking about injuries and claiming—Reverend Charlton Fillmore. It's evident from Miranda's account that her perception of Lily's injury had been totally transformed by a religious conversion that occurred after she filed her lawsuit. As a born-again Christian, Miranda now took primary responsibility for the accident, rather than blaming the automobile dealership: "In the last two years, I accepted Christ as my savior, and I realize now that she really had no business being out there by that garbage can. If somebody had been watching her, like I should have been, she wouldn't have gotten hurt."

Miranda had also come to believe that the claim for money damages was morally wrong and produced nothing but trouble: "I really feel now that I shouldn't have done it, because the money, even though it wasn't very much, it caused a lot of damage between my husband and I. Because we fought over it constantly. . . . It's just been a big heartache, a big headache, you know, really. Maybe I'm wrong, but I feel that it wasn't the right thing to do. . . . [I]f I had to do it over again, I wouldn't." She came to understand that the Christian response to an injury, even one as serious as Lily's, would have been to lump rather than claim. Miranda now believed that her concern about future financial difficulties had been misguided, because God would have provided.

Miranda's new view of Lily's injury clearly reflected the influence of Reverend Fillmore rather than that of her ex-husband. For Reverend Fillmore, the essence of Christianity is acceptance and forgiveness, not rights assertion: "That's the heart of Christianity probably, and that is forgiveness." He taught Miranda that her un-Christian, selfish, and materialistic quest for compensation represented the very opposite of forgiveness. Plaintiffs in injury cases delude themselves. They erroneously believe that their troubles can be solved by a claim for money damages. Instead, in Reverend Fillmore's words, they need to set things right with God:

> That void that man is always grasping and searching for. Some try to do it through searching for money, the almighty dollar. . . . That emptiness, that void that every man feels, can only be filled through God. . . . There is more than just making money. There is more than just trying to do right. There is a right relationship with God that can give purpose to this life and assurance in the life to come, and that can come by inviting Jesus Christ into your heart.

Claiming, disputing, and litigation are not the answer. "If we first of all get first things straightened out, and that is our relationship with God and is our help from God, all of these other things will fall into order."

If Miranda had experienced her religious conversion two years sooner, it's very likely that her response to Lily's injury would have been influenced by Reverend Fillmore rather than by her ex-husband. Her initial inclination to lump rather than claim would have been reinforced. She would never have approached a lawyer and instead would have turned to prayer and forgiveness. Her attention would have shifted from money concerns to "first things," and she would have asked for help from God rather than the courts. As her relationships with others shifted during this period in her life, so did her perception of Lily's injury and the most appropriate way for her to respond to it. Temporarily swayed by her husband's influence in the direction of claiming, she was soon convinced by Reverend Fillmore to adopt a perspective favoring lumping. Her antilitigious thinking was brought into line with the most common viewpoint not only in Sander County but in American society generally.

HOW INFLUENCE OCCURS

How does one human being influence the decision making of another? Sometimes the effect is so obvious that it requires little explanation. A parent may influence her teenager's decision to decline an invitation to a weeknight party by telling him that he shouldn't go. The child in a sense "decides" to stay home, but his decision reflects the parent's preferences and not his own. Parental influence in such instances is powerful because of the inherent authority of moms and dads, not to mention their power to withhold their child's allowance and future privileges. Similarly, an employer may order his subordinates to contribute to a local politician's mayoral campaign. Although the employees ostensibly make their own decision, they are clearly influenced by the fear of getting fired or being denied a promotion.

The influence of others can, however, take less explicit forms. An abusive husband can create a relationship of dominance and submission such that all of his wife's decisions reflect his wishes, even when there is no overt threat of retaliation. This may well have been the case when Miranda Compton decided to bring a lawsuit on behalf of her daughter Lily. She later admitted that her husband had persuaded her to make a choice that she came to regret.

But it would be a mistake to limit our understanding of influence to those situations where one person tells another, "You should do this" or "You must do that." Influence can take many forms that are far more subtle and indirect. Groups of birds and fish rely on what scientists call "quorum decision-making" when they collectively and seemingly spontaneously change direction and speed.[6] Similarly, individual humans make decisions as part of their social network, even when they act without explicit direction. Their decision making reflects their identity—their sense of who they are within a collectivity. Human identity isn't formed in solitude. We *are* our relationships.

We have already seen that a key element of cognition is what Damasio calls the *autobiographical self,* an internal narrative that runs continually in our minds, like a television set that is never turned off.[7] The autobiographical self operates nonconsciously and automatically, but it can also become the focus of slower and more self-aware thinking. At such moments, people deliberately narrate portions of their lives to themselves—and very often to others as well.

Sharing the internal narrative with other people is critically important. The autobiographical self is both social and interactional. Telling our stories to others, and hearing their responses, is what makes us human. As psychologist Jerome Bruner has observed, the self does not exist apart from our relationships with others but is "distributed" throughout one's relational networks. Bruner compares the distributed self to filing notes in different locations, making it possible for a person to look up different parts of his or her knowledge in different places. Similarly, by distributing aspects of one's life and experiences among different people in our relational network, the "[s]elf becomes enmeshed in a net of others."[8]

The autobiographical stories we tell others and ourselves are never fixed. They aren't like the printed pages of a book. They are more like the riffs of a jazz musician, infinitely malleable and responsive to the expressions of others in the group. These narratives change constantly in response to new events. And we tell the stories differently depending on our purpose, our audience, and our state of mind. The autobiographical accounts we create for ourselves and others are not just a record of the past; they are also maps for the future. They prepare us to make new choices. If I tell my life story to bolster my identity as *this* kind of person, I prepare myself for *that* course of action.[9]

What does all this have to do with injuries and the victim's decision making? A personal injury becomes a significant event in most people's autobiographical narrative. They integrate the mishap instantly into their life story, and they may describe it to others, including friends, family, and coworkers, as well as professional service providers. Each retelling provides the injured person an opportunity for revision, and each listener offers comments or reactions that alter the original perception. The listeners' responses create a recursive loop. The injury victim is likely to revise the original narrative and then offer it to other listeners, who in turn provide their own feedback. Thus, the injury narrative is continually revised as a result of interactions with important others, and the injury victim's thoughts and plans change accordingly. In this process, we may find keys to the decision making that follows an injury—and a better understanding of the predominant tendency to absorb most injuries without lodging a complaint or seeking a remedy.

There can be little doubt that interactions with third parties are capable of changing one's thoughts and self-conceptions concerning important matters, including how to respond to a personal injury. We saw this happen in the story Miranda Compton told about her daughter's injury and its reinterpretation during her interactions first with her ex-husband and then with Reverend Fillmore. It appears that Reverend Fillmore became a supremely important person in Miranda's life. She listened to him and, it seems, he listened to her as well. She probably shared with him the story of Lily's accident and her decision to consult a lawyer. He undoubtedly responded with the same observations he offered when I later interviewed him. He must have told Miranda that the emptiness and unhappiness in her life could not be filled with money. To accept God is to forgive others for their wrongdoing. The solution to her distress could never be achieved through tort law but only by "inviting Jesus Christ into your heart."

Miranda Compton's give-and-take with Reverend Fillmore changed her autobiographical narrative. That is, it changed the story she told about Lily's accident. Even more importantly, it changed her *self*. By interacting with others who were important to her, she became a different person with a different narrative running through her consciousness. In her new narrative, law and legal rights were not only unimportant, they were barriers to salvation.

It's no exaggeration to say that reality itself is shared, that humans *collectively* construct their understanding of the world in which they live. A line of scholarship known as "shared reality theory" posits that people collaborate in their construction of reality. They figure out what others think and feel about the world around them, and they try to align their inner thoughts and emotions accordingly:

Shared reality includes explicit agreement and consensus, although it is not limited to them. Shared reality may be expressed or tacit, newly negotiated or long assumed. Shared reality processes may operate either consciously or unconsciously, achieved through effortful deliberation or automatic information processing.[10]

The urge to share understandings of reality with others is especially strong when people must confront "potentially anxiety-arousing situations."[11] This point is particularly relevant to the problem of *injuries*, which, to put it mildly, tend to arouse the anxiety of victims. Establishing a common viewpoint would offer reassurance and a sense of security to injury victims as they struggle with the aftereffects of their traumatic experience. The need to forge a shared reality in these troubling circumstances must be especially acute, and the opinions of other people would seem to provide the victims with the most reliable guidance for future action.

The durability of shared reality perspectives, according to this line of research, depends on the number of relationships and their strength and stability. When there is a strong motivation to preserve the relationships over time, then the version of reality they generate is more likely to endure.[12] For injury victims, this means that interactions with their closest friends and family members will produce a shared understanding of the accident, why it happened, and what should be done about it—and this understanding is likely to have a powerful effect on the victims' thoughts and actions for quite a long time, because of the strength and stability of the relationships.

WHY THE INFLUENCE OF OTHERS
TENDS TO INCREASE LUMPING

Thus, there is substantial evidence that the influence of others can cause people to change their perceptions of important events such as injuries, as well as their responses to them.

But why do interactions with other people contribute to cognitive shifts in the direction of lumping rather than claiming? How exactly do social interactions help to explain the central problem of this book—the dog that doesn't bark in the night?

We have already seen that the social environment is filled with ideas, images, and norms that tend to favor lumping over claiming in injury cases. It's not difficult to imagine the mechanism by which a prolumping perspective gets communicated through the victim's interaction with other people, as was the case eventually with Miranda Compton. Each encounter, each conversation, replicates at the micro level the same anticlaiming bias that is found in the environment at the macro level.[13] When we open ourselves to the influence of others, the result is neither random nor symmetrical. Our interactions provide opportunities for dominant ideologies—such as the ideology of individual responsibility and antilitigiousness—to impress themselves on the perceptions and decisions of individual actors and structure their thoughts.

Psychologists tell us that people interpret their experiences and determine their behavior by using *schemas*, which are "mental frameworks" that contain "information relevant to self, other people, specific situations or events."[14] Schemas that help us to understand particular kinds of events and offer predictable ways to respond are known as *scripts*: "A script is a structure that describes appropriate sequences of events in a particular context."[15] Schemas and scripts take shape within specific social environments and reflect the ideas, images, and norms that prevail in those settings. When injury victims interact with other people, these mental frameworks are reinforced. Predominant scripts give meaning to the injurious experience and suggest an appropriate path to pursue. The victims' friends and acquaintances remind them that there is an obvious, "natural," and correct way to interpret their experiences and respond to them.

The most influential scripts for injury victims are those that favor lumping rather than claiming. Interactions with people who are important in their lives are most likely to reinforce scripts of conflict avoidance and not the pursuit of compensation or assertion of rights. Shared reality theorists provide one indication why that might be the case. Asserting a claim and engaging in litigation are behaviors that are often attributed to social outsiders, troublemakers, or misfits. Researchers have found that, in constructing shared realities, "individuals shift their attitudes away from disliked or socially peripheral others."[16] In fact, one study suggests that politically conservative ideologies, such as tort reform, may tend to emerge more often as winners in this process because of the clarity and simplicity of their content:

> [W]e think that shared reality motives might lead disproportionately to conservative, system-justifying outcomes because of communicative advantages associated with conservative cognitive and rhetorical styles. . . . Because conservative rhetoric and ideology tends to be simpler, more consistent, and less ambiguous on average than liberal rhetoric and ideology, relational motives for shared reality may generally elicit relatively conservative attitudes.[17]

If correct, this theory makes it easier to understand why an injury victim's interactions with others would tend most often to generate a response that conforms to the ideology of individual responsibility rather than claiming. This certainly proved to be the case for Miranda Compton. Her initial decision to bring a claim, influenced by an ex-husband who was a social outcast, was in the end overtaken by a more conservative, simple, and unambiguous perspective that resembled not only the ideology of her minister and his congregation but also that of most mainstream Sander County residents.

A somewhat different explanation of how others influence victims to lump emerges from the ideas about human cognition discussed in chapter 4. As we saw there, humans love to take cognitive shortcuts when they process new information and arrive at important decisions. Psychologists call these shortcuts *heuristics*, which are "simple 'rules of thumb' which we use to make complex inferences by simplifying and streamlining the amount of information available."[18] Heuristics are highly efficient, since people are constantly bombarded by stimuli and data. They facilitate both nonconscious and conscious mental activities and help the mind to operate smoothly with minimal effort. But cognitive processes are also vulnerable to distortion, mistake, and bias, which psychologists take delight in cataloging. The hundreds of psych experiments illustrating people's sometimes laughable fallibility remind us that to err is indeed human.

Some of the cognitive biases most likely to affect the perceptions and decisions of injury victims are associated with the influence third persons have on human subjectivity. And it's easy to see how they might lead toward lumping rather than claiming. For example, the *priming effect* causes people to form judgments and act in ways that reflect their prior exposure to images, concepts, or ideas, even if the exposure occurs subconsciously or is seemingly irrelevant to the matter at hand.[19] People are so suggestible that implanting a concept in their minds, such as the concept of old age, can lead them unconsciously to walk around the room like an elderly person.[20] People's sense of self can change merely by positioning them near bystanders with different types of physical appearance.[21] This sort of suggestibility is highly relevant to the social influences that could lead injury victims to lump. It seems probable that interacting with other people would most often prime injury victims to adopt a negative perspective toward asserting claims for compensation, since that's the most widespread perspective one is likely to encounter in our society. If you have heard your friends over the years condemn the socially destructive behavior of personal injury plaintiffs, and then you suffer an injury yourself, you have been primed to lump rather than claim.

A second cognitive bias is the *mere exposure effect*, which produces a favorable response to familiar words or images only because the individual has experienced them previously.[22] This type of bias, too, is likely to be associated with the individual's interpersonal interactions. Certain ideas or concepts tend to be expressed repeatedly within any relational network. For example, an individual might hear friends and family talk on many occasions about the regrettable tendency of Americans to sue one another at the drop of a hat. Even if these comments lack any basis in reality, their mere repetition could affect cognition of new events such as injuries. They might, for example, instill the ethical notion that injury victims should be stoic in the face of pain and suffering and should not be quick to assert claims.

A third cognitive bias is the *availability heuristic*, which, according to Daniel Kahneman, leads people to make judgments about the frequency of a category based, illogically, on how easy it is for them to retrieve examples from their memory.[23] We could imagine that injury victims might have friends who repeatedly talk about greedy injury victims and nonmeritorious lawsuits. They would, as a result, tend to estimate that frivolous personal injury litigation is very common regardless of the evidence to the contrary. It's alarming to think that a tidal wave of tort actions has swept over our society. The influence of friends would instill an exaggerated sense of crisis in our courts and reinforce a bias against taking any action that might associate the injury victim with the perceived excesses of tort claimants.

These three examples show how interactions with third parties can trigger cognitive biases that make lumping appear the most obvious and appropriate response to an injury. It's not just that lumping comes to seem natural. The influence of friends can actually convince us that lumping is *morally preferable* to claiming. Even though people tend to be very reluctant to change their moral judgments, the influence of others can cause them to do so. As Jonathan Haidt observes:

> We make our first judgments rapidly, and we are dreadful at seeking out evidence that might disconfirm those initial judgments. Yet friends can do for us what we cannot do for ourselves: they can challenge us, giving us reasons and arguments . . . that sometimes trigger new intuitions, thereby making it possible for us to change our minds. . . . For most of us, it's not every day or even every month that we change our mind about a moral issue without any prompting from anyone else.
>
> Far more common than such private mind changing is social influence.[24]

It seems reasonable, then, to suggest that social interactions tend to have an asymmetrical influence on injury victims, although there are certainly some counterexamples—occasions when friends advise injury victims to consult a lawyer or press a claim.[25] Far more often, however, the influence of others is likely to encourage victims to lump rather than claim. These interactions occur in social settings where the antilitigation ideology of individual responsibility usually holds sway.[26] Because the ideology of lumping is more popular in American society than the ideology of claiming and litigating, third-party influence is most likely to influence individuals not to pursue a demand for compensation.

THE INFLUENCE OF PROFESSIONALS

Our discussion of third-party influence on lumping has focused on friends, family, and coworkers rather than professionals. There is a good reason for this. As we have seen, the vast majority of injury victims never take any steps at all to demand compensation. Most nascent claims come to an end before they ever get near the office of a lawyer, government official, or other potentially helpful professional. This silent majority of injury victims in America represents most of the people whose actions—or inactions—need to be explained.

But let's imagine a potential plaintiff who does not fall within this large group of nonactivists. Suppose this imaginary injury victim is among the tiny minority who actually do "take some action" (in the words of the RAND study). Does the influence of other people also affect them? The RAND study found that, out of every ten "activists," seven consult an attorney, four deal directly with the injurer's insurance company, and two have direct contact with the injurer (these numbers add up to more than ten because some individuals pursued more than one option). Clearly, these potential plaintiffs have had an entirely different set of social interactions in comparison to those who took no action at all. How did the influence of others affect *their* decision making? Let's consider the influence of legal professionals, insurance company representatives, and the injurers themselves.

One might assume that the influence of lawyers on members of the activist minority of injury victims was invariably in the direction of claiming rather than lumping. Surprisingly, however, this is not the case. A substantial number of the potential plaintiffs who knocked on lawyers' doors were, as a result, influenced to lump rather than claim—and that's exactly what they ended up doing.

How can this be true? Don't personal injury lawyers *always* encourage prospective clients to claim? Contrary to what we might expect, there is evidence that injury victims who consult lawyers are very likely to be discouraged from pursuing a claim. Herbert M. Kritzer's study of contingency fee lawyers in Wisconsin found that they turned down 66 percent of all the civil cases that came through their doors.[27] Of course, many of these cases were rejected on the merits. The lawyers recognized that there was simply no valid legal claim and properly refused them.

But lawyers declined other cases even when they thought they did have merit. Those were the cases that wouldn't yield a sufficient damage award and attorney's fee, even if the claims were valid. In Kritzer's study, 19 percent of the cases declined were turned away because of "inadequate damages" (and an additional 13 percent of the declined cases had inadequate damages plus possible lack of liability). In addition, lawyers viewed some of the declined cases as outside their area of practice (11 percent) or refused them for other reasons (11 percent), such as the difficult personality of the client or potential conflicts of interest.[28]

In short, Kritzer's study suggests that interaction with lawyers more often leads the potential plaintiff to lump or seek another lawyer rather than to claim. Significantly, the lawyers' encouragement to lump occurs even in many cases that the legal system might find meritorious.

But surely this kind of influence toward lumping doesn't occur when the potential plaintiff communicates with the injurer's insurance company rather than an attorney. Isn't a contact with the other side's insurer almost by definition claiming rather than lumping? Well, not exactly. It's true, of course, that whenever compensation is offered or demanded, the topic of discussion is the victim's potential claim against the injurer's policy. Yet we know that insurance companies often try to move quickly and aggressively to offer victims a money settlement precisely because they want to *prevent* them from claiming. The insurance company and not the potential plaintiff initiates these discussions. They know that the more quickly they can put a check in the victim's hands, the less likely it is the victim will demand anything more or consider a lawsuit. Because this process is set in motion by the potential defendant, it can't accurately be described as "claiming" (although lurking in the background is the claim the victims might bring if a solution can't be found).

These speedy settlement practices sometimes catch injury victims unprepared. Although the payments may seem generous, or even an unexpected windfall, they typically involve smaller amounts than the victims might obtain if they lodged a formal claim with the help of an attorney and won at trial. The insurance company's offer may understate the value of the victim's losses, particularly future expenses, and may omit pain and suffering entirely. In these instances, interaction with an insurance company doesn't exactly influence victims to lump their losses, but it does suppress or weaken potential claims. Rather than claiming by the victim, or encouragement to claim, the process could be better described as the preemption of claiming.

Even direct contact with the injurers themselves may influence victims to engage in lumping rather than claiming—if the injurers handle the interaction properly. The injurer who voices compassion and regret may cause the potential plaintiff not to claim. Research by Jennifer K. Robbennolt found that an injurer's full apology expressing sympathy and taking responsibility for the accident had a powerful effect on her subjects. The apology led them to attribute positive moral qualities to the injurer, to believe he would be more careful in the future, to decrease their anger, and to feel sympathy for him. In addition, her subjects were much more receptive to a settlement offer after a full apology was offered.[29]

The powerful effects of apology have been well documented in medical malpractice cases. When hospitals adopt a policy of disclosing errors and issuing apologies to patients they have harmed, the number of claims drops dramatically. A doctor's apology satisfies many injury victims and disarms others. Although the apology is often accompanied by an offer of compensation, the disclosure-and-apology strategy tends to reduce hospitals' legal expenses substantially.[30] Whereas tort lawyers customarily instruct injurers not to communicate with their victims, many have now come to realize—at least in medical malpractice cases—that interaction between injurer and victim is more likely to promote lumping or more limited claiming than is silence. In this sense, too, the influence of others can moderate the urge to claim and sometimes eliminate claiming altogether.

CONCLUSION

It's a mistake to think of the choice between claiming and lumping as an individualized process. It's not enough to analyze the decisions of the injury victim, even when the broader physical and cultural environments are taken into account. Injury victims, like most humans, are embedded in social networks that influence their thoughts and actions. Even if traumatic injuries sometimes reduce their social interactions, most injury victims still view themselves as someone else's child or parent, brother or sister, friend, spouse, or coworker. These relationships make us who we are, and they also shape our decisions. It's necessary to account for the influence of other people if we are to understand fully how injury victims choose to claim, lump, or engage in some other response to their injury.

In theory, the influence of others could operate either to increase claims or to increase lumping. But in practice, it appears that our interactions with other people tend most often to encourage lumping. There are several reasons for this asymmetrical effect:

- Since the predominant social and cultural norms in most settings discourage injury victims from aggressive claiming behavior, it's most likely that a third party who interacts with an injury victim will share these norms and influence the injury victim in the direction of lumping.
- The influence of others can be direct or indirect, deliberate or unwitting. Indirectly, an injury victim's thoughts and actions can be affected when other people help to instill schemas and scripts consistent with lumping or when they reinforce cognitive biases that discourage claiming.
- Direct and explicit discussions with third parties are likely to make injury victims more aware of negative social stereotypes associated with injury victims who claim or sue. Third parties tend to take a more objective "external" view of the matter. The "internal" view of the injury victim is, according to some researchers, likely to be overly focused on specifics and unique details of the accident that has just occurred, while missing the big picture.[31] A third party who takes a more distanced view may be more inclined to see the costs and negative consequences of claiming and to focus on the

deleterious effects litigation has on society as a whole. They may feel protective toward the injury victim or sorry for her and try to shield her from further distress.

- Even if the third parties happen to be lawyers, insurance company representatives, or the injurers themselves, interacting with them still may discourage claiming and encourage lumping. Among the small minority of injury victims who take initial steps toward "doing something," most of them don't end up claiming. When they deal with lawyers, insurance adjusters, or the injurers themselves, victims tend to be influenced by those very interactions to abandon their claims, reduce them, or accept a relatively limited preemptive offer. Researchers have found that apologies by the injurers are especially potent, causing injury victims to think more highly of the injurer and to reduce their claims or lump their losses.

In all of these ways, influential friends, relatives, coworkers, and professionals can affect the decisions of injury victims. Together, they construct a version of reality that explains what has happened and what should be done about it. This is a collective process, not an individual one. And the nature of these interactions is such that their influence far more often encourages lumping, or a limitation of one's expectations, rather than claiming or litigation. In this way, generalized cultural norms and ideas become concretized, and abstract concerns about litigiousness are translated into actual decisions to minimize one's demands and absorb the costs and consequences of injuries.

TEN   CONCLUSION

||||||||||||||||||||||||||||||||||||||||||||||||||||||||||||||||||||||||||||||||||||||||||||||

This book seeks to answer a question—Why is it that injury victims seldom press claims against their injurers and almost never take legal action? I have argued that this is the question we should be answering, *not* why are Americans so litigious, or how can we reduce frivolous personal injury claims, or what can we do about out-of-control damage awards? To get the right answers, we must ask the right questions. That's particularly true of personal injuries and the law, a field in which the wrong questions have produced a great many irrelevant and even harmful answers.

The question at the heart of this book may seem counterintuitive, but it is in fact critically important. If most injury victims never pursue their potential claims, if the law plays little direct role in their lives, then our most basic assumptions about injuries and the justice system must be reexamined. Contrary to popular belief, the vast majority of injury victims rely only on their own resources, on friends and family, on government welfare programs, or on private insurance to cover, at most, a portion of their medical expenses—but not their pain and suffering, the diminished quality of their life, the loss of future earnings, or the burdens imposed on caretakers. In light of that sobering reality, we really do need to explain why "lumping" is the predominant response to injuries in American society.

Yet this is a question that has been largely ignored. Or, more accurately, the question has been obscured by a specter, the apparition of the litigious American, which has dominated public discourse about injuries in our society and distorted our debate about tort law and tort reform. This fictitious figure, like the "man who wasn't there" in the popular rhyme, must be banished if we ever hope to have a sensible discussion about America's injury problem and the capacity or incapacity of tort law to address it:

> Yesterday, upon the stair,
> I met a man who wasn't there
> He wasn't there again today
> I wish, I wish he'd go away. . . .[1]

The myth of the litigious American has led policy makers to consider solutions that fail to address the real problems of injury compensation, deterrence, and social justice in our society. To answer the more pertinent question, why injured Americans are so distinctly *non*litigious, I have emulated Sherlock Holmes in "Silver Blaze," who found it necessary to explain why the dog didn't bark during the night when a murder occurred. There are actually many clues out there to solve our mystery, but they've not been heeded. I found them buried in studies from very diverse fields, ranging from psychology to neurology, from rehabilitation science to anesthesiology, from history to nursing, from sociology to linguistics, anthropology, and cultural studies.

Readers may have experienced some disquiet when a torts professor—albeit one affiliated with the interdisciplinary field of law and society—announced in the early pages of this book that he intended to launch such a wide-ranging investigation. I cannot claim expertise in each of these disciplines—perhaps no one can—but, like an early explorer, I have tried to map the terrain and have returned with indications that future expeditions will discover many treasures. Even this initial foray has provided a number of answers and suggested a new model for research. In the process, I hope it has encouraged others to ask new and better questions.

In the remainder of this conclusion, I will summarize the answers I've uncovered to explain the missing plaintiff in injury cases, discuss the reasons why all of this matters, point out some of the existing "work-arounds" for the problem of the reluctant plaintiff, and conclude with a general call for a cultural shift in our public discussions of injuries and the law.

MYSTERY SOLVED: WHY LUMPING IS SO COMMON

This investigation of the mystery of the missing plaintiff has proceeded from one type of clue to the next. After documenting in chapter 2 that there was indeed an absence of claims to be accounted for, I proceeded in chapter 3 to take a close look at the actual experience of injury victims, not the two-dimensional characters of social and legal theorists but the flesh-and-blood humans who suffer the pain and trauma of physical harm. It became clear that, when real people experience physical injuries, their lives, thoughts, and emotions are profoundly disrupted and compromised. Paradoxically, they are often overcome by guilt and self-blame. They are seldom sturdy enough, mentally or physically, to pursue a claim against someone else.

To understand the impact of such events on their decision making, chapter 4 explored the most recent studies of how the mind works, particularly in relation to a body that has suffered pain and trauma. These studies explained that cognition is organically connected to one's body, and therefore an injury that damages or impairs the body is bound to affect how the victim thinks about the experience and makes decisions afterward. By this point, it had become evident that I needed an entirely new model of injury perception and response—a model less dependent on the "rational actor" and more cognizant of the interconnections linking humans to their physical and social environments and to influential other people. The presentation of the new model was the subject of chapter 5.

Equipped with a more sophisticated and empirically grounded understanding of cognition, and taking better account of the social and cultural context of injury victims, I was able, in chapters 6 through 9, to identify a number of reasons why injuries so rarely lead to claims. Here, then, are eight of the most significant explanations for the predominance of lumping among injury victims in America:

First, the disabling effects of an injury, especially a traumatic one, reduce the likelihood that victims will demand compensation from the injurer or will seek help from an attorney. Serious injuries tend to create a sense of existential change and identity confusion, an inability to think clearly and act decisively while in pain, a sense of social isolation, a failure of language, and self-blame. Pain medications also interfere with rational thought, and fatigue saps the energy needed to pursue a complaint. All of these physical and mental aftereffects of physical injuries tend to diminish the likelihood that the victim will lodge a claim.

Second, our society for the most part holds a negative view of claiming by injury victims. The whining, greedy, deceitful plaintiff is a familiar figure in our popular culture, the subject of films, newspaper articles, and late night comedy. Few people want to be identified with this questionable character. Highly effective and well-funded public relations campaigns by tort reformers have reinforced the negative view of injury claimants, which is now widely accepted throughout American society. Injury victims who consider claiming or suing run the risk that they will associate themselves with powerful negative stereotypes. Their friends and family may disagree with the decision to pursue a claim, and the decision may expose them to disapproval or even ridicule within their social networks. Rather than buck these strong cultural currents, many are willing to lump their losses.

Third, because we "think with our bodies," injury victims must consider their harm—and weigh their potential response—with the very instrument that has suffered damage. The paradox of viewing an experience through a lens clouded by the experience itself makes people's cognition particularly vulnerable to mistakes and biases. Much of our thinking, even in the absence of an injury, is nonconscious rather than deliberate, self-aware, and rational. Nonconscious cognition, though crucially important for our decision making, is far from rational. It's very misleading to imagine an injury victim making carefully balanced decisions after objectively weighing the costs and benefits of claiming versus lumping. Most human cognition fails to match this idealized model, especially after the pain and trauma of an injury. The victims' "irrational" thinking, for reasons examined in detail throughout the book, encourages them to lump their losses even in circumstances when an objective and rational analysis of costs and benefits might suggest they should demand compensation.

Fourth, the concept of "injury" is itself a cultural construct. Painful events that could be considered injuries—such as male infant circumcisions—are not necessarily perceived as injurious, because they are constructed as normal or natural. Sometimes painful events are considered beneficial and not harmful.

If it is believed that there is no injury, the likelihood of bringing a claim is all but eliminated.

Fifth, even when painful events are perceived as injuries, they can be *naturalized* in a way that precludes the possibility of bringing a claim. Injuries are viewed as natural when they are considered a normal part of the physical or social environment, and they become unnatural only when some safer alternative is widely accepted. Until the emergence and widespread approval of the safer option, however, claims appear absurd. Thus, injuries on stairways were considered natural and inevitable—and most likely the fault of the victim's own carelessness or infirmity—until safety engineers pointed out that safer stair designs could eliminate a great many of these very common accidents.

Sixth, many injuries result from deliberate choices by manufacturers or service providers, but those choices are invisible to injury victims. Products can actually "encode" assumptions about the number and severity of risks that it is acceptable to impose on consumers. If these choices and assumptions are not recognized, however, it's unlikely that injury victims will challenge them and blame the injurers. For example, it was long assumed that the risk of injuring or killing children while backing up was inherent in motor vehicles rather than the result of a decision not to provide rearview cameras. When children were injured, parents blamed themselves or concluded it was no one's fault—until the consensus changed, and automobiles without cameras began to be viewed as inadequate. Prior to that shift, however, injuries were simply lumped because they were viewed as unavoidable. The decision to impose this risk on consumers and their children remained hidden and few claims were brought against manufacturers.

Seventh, to the extent that human nature, culture, or predominant social values suppress the perception of *causal links* in injury cases, victims are unlikely to attribute responsibility to another person and pursue a claim for compensation. For certain kinds of injuries or illnesses, the cause may be genuinely unknown. Human wrongdoing is just one possibility. Lumping of such harms almost goes without saying. For other kinds of injuries, wrongdoing is more obvious, but the recognition of a causal connection depends on the observer's cultural perspective, economic interests, or religious orientation. Causation, although seemingly an objective "fact," is actually the result of a subjective process that is vulnerable to all of the cognitive and cultural impediments to claiming that we have already enumerated. Needless to say, in the countless instances where there is no perceived causal connection to some wrongdoer, lodging a claim simply makes no sense.

Eighth, other people play a crucial role in the decision making of the injury victim. Although sometimes a friend or relative may advise a victim to see an attorney, more often interactions with others lead injury victims toward lumping. Friends and relatives tend to reflect the societal consensus that it's bad to claim, and the victim who demands compensation will become a social pariah. Friends can see clearly what an outraged injury victim may temporarily overlook—that the aggravation and condemnation associated with lodging a claim won't be worth it. It's better to do the best one can and get on with one's life. Furthermore, even when friends or acquaintances don't explicitly advise against claiming, the process of shared reality construction means that injury victims' perceptions are shaped within their social networks and reflect the values of other people, not just the victim alone. Chances are that any grouping of people in our society will share the predominant negative view of claiming and will consider lumping to be the preferred response. And when injury victims make the atypical decision to consult a lawyer, there is a high probability that even this interaction with a professional advocate will influence them to abandon the claim.

These are among the most important explanations for the predominance of lumping that were uncovered in this investigation. Together, they present a picture of an asymmetrical set of social, cultural, and cognitive factors that mitigate against claiming. Taking them into account, it becomes easier to understand why Americans so seldom lodge a claim after suffering an injury—even a severe injury. The odds are stacked against confronting the injurer in any way, and they get even steeper when it comes to suing in a court of law. The rare individual who defies those odds in order to gain the benefits of a successful legal action must also be prepared to pay a very stiff price for the decision in loss of esteem among friends and members of the community.

WHY THE PREDOMINANCE OF LUMPING MATTERS

Sometimes it seems that tort law is like the host who threw a party and nobody came. Why does this matter? What difference does it make if claims for compensation are voiced by only 10 percent of all injury victims or by 100 percent? I have tried to be clear that this book is not a brief in support of the current tort law system. I do not necessarily believe that we would be a happier, more prosperous, or cohesive society if the percentage of injury victims who bring lawsuits could be greatly increased. We might find the results too inimical to our norms of civility, respect, and interpersonal flexibility. A dramatic rise in the amount of tort litigation could create a culture of adversarialism and selfishness that would seriously degrade our quality of life.

Nevertheless, I contend that failure to recognize the frequency of lumping among injury victims results in serious consequences that should be addressed. Whether we favor more or fewer lawsuits, most of us would agree that the self-professed goals of tort law are valid and worth striving for. Those goals include the compensation of victims for all their losses (not just medical expenses), the deterrence and reduction of injuries, the distribution of injury costs among a broad group of people, and the enforcement of norms of fairness and justice.

All of these goals are admirable, but they can be achieved through tort law only if injury victims actually bring claims against their injurers. Tort law is a reactive instrument of social policy. It does not go out into neighborhoods or the marketplace to identify violations. Rather, it waits patiently in the courthouse for aggrieved individuals to bring their cases to justice and set the legal machinery in motion. In short, claiming is what activates tort law. When injury cases are lumped, tort law remains dormant and cannot achieve its stated goals. The predominance of lumping over claiming in injury cases has three extremely important social and legal consequences:

1. The Predominance of Lumping Distorts Tort Law

American tort law professes the ability to do something about the injury problem. But it can't *compensate* victims effectively if it reimburses a mere handful of the millions who are harmed each year. It can't *deter* injurers if it leaves most of them free to engage in further irresponsible behavior with little likelihood they will suffer any sanction. It can't *redistribute losses* if claims are never presented. And it can't *enact moral justice* in more than a tiny fraction of the many cases in which injurers unfairly harmed their victims. It's true, of course, that informal settlements are often negotiated outside the courts in the shadow of tort law. Yet we have learned that such settlements occur relatively infrequently. Since approximately nine out of ten injury victims never lodge any claim or consult a lawyer, they seldom put themselves in a position to negotiate a settlement. And when liability insurance companies occasionally issue unilateral preemptive offers to injury victims, they apply different metrics from those a plaintiffs' attorney or trial jury would use to calculate damages.[2] In most injury cases, then, the core purposes of tort law are largely irrelevant.

It might be argued that some of tort law's goals can be realized if even a very small percentage of victims lodge claims. This is doubtful. I suppose it's possible that tort law can exercise its deterrent effect simply because potential defendants overestimate the likelihood that they'll be sued. Michael J. Saks raises this possibility when he muses that tort law, despite its infrequent use, could be "a mouse with an otherworldly roar."[3] But it seems far more likely that tort law is just an ordinary mouse uttering unimpressive squeaks in response to risky behavior that threatens our safety. Deterrence theorists have long assumed that injury victims will present valid claims for adjudication—as opposed to simply lumping. For example, in a classic article on the "Hand formula," which is tort law's most frequently cited cost-benefit rubric, Richard Posner explains the deterrent function of tort law by asserting that a rational enterprise achieves optimal levels of safety by balancing the cost of injury prevention against the probability and cost of injuries: "When the cost of accidents is less than the cost of prevention, a rational profit-maximizing enterprise will pay tort judgments to the accident victims rather than incur the larger cost of avoiding liability."[4] But what if the enterprise is seldom asked to "pay tort judgments to accident victims"? What if most accident victims never bring claims? What happens then to the enterprise's calculation of acceptable risk levels? Surely wide-scale lumping will radically weaken the deterrent effect that theorists like Posner have long ascribed to tort law.

If rights violations are seldom met with rights claims, then the basic premise of any reactive legal regime is flawed. Theorists can talk about tort law's lofty goals, but they must recognize that these goals will be difficult to attain as long as most individuals are simply unwilling to engage in adversarial legalism. If we as a society value the goals of compensation, deterrence, loss distribution, and corrective justice, we will have to find other ways to achieve them rather than relying on tort law as it currently operates.

2. The Absence of Claims Weakens Tort Law's Early Warning Function

Closely related to the goals of compensation, deterrence, loss distribution, and corrective justice is a function tort law has long served in American society—it flags new kinds of risky behavior and unsafe products and services. Before government agencies can target new sources of harm, individual plaintiffs and their lawyers bring them to the attention of the legal system through private claims for damages. Tort law provides a signaling function for state agencies and officials and for the public at large. A tort lawsuit can announce, "Here is a new problem worthy of attention, and here is what a judge and jury concluded about the seriousness of the risk."

The signaling function of tort law, however, can be weakened or eliminated entirely if most injury victims never consult a lawyer or bring a claim. In fact, lawyers themselves may refuse to pursue novel claims when the legal rules have been changed to discourage litigation and limit damages. Those who favor lumping and think there should be more of it need to explain how they propose to replace tort law's function as an early warning system.

Tort law not only signals new sources of harm, it also plays a key role in the cultural construction of injury. As we have seen, the very concept of an injury can shift over time with new understandings of appropriate social behavior and acceptable risk. Sexual harassment in the workplace was once viewed as normal behavior. Lung cancer caused by cigarettes was once viewed as bad luck or the responsibility of the smoker alone. Negligent conduct that caused psychological but not physical harm was once viewed as noncompensable. As judges and juries decided cases involving claims for such harms, their decisions contributed to cultural shifts. The meanings of "injury" and "responsibility" were expanded and popular understandings of appropriate and acceptable behavior underwent change. To the extent that claiming is discouraged, litigation of new forms of injury will be curtailed. Tort law will play a limited role in reshaping social norms.

3. Injuries without Remedies Are Bad for Our Society

The need to supplement or replace tort law is particularly urgent when we recognize the tens of thousands of injury victims who, by choice or circumstance, are left to fend for themselves. Injuries fall disproportionately on people with fewer resources, and they tend to impoverish their victims. The cost of injuries can't be measured only in terms of medical bills. Injuries can also stunt careers and force the victims into worse paying jobs or even unemployment. Injuries have emotional and psychological repercussions that can prove more debilitating than physical harms. Depression, fear, anxiety, and social isolation, if unaddressed, can change lives permanently for the worse.

Injuries without remedies create a social underclass whose needs must be met, if at all, by their families or by government programs. The costs that should in theory be borne by the injurers and their insurance companies instead become a dead weight dragging down the injury victims and those around them. These costs add to the tax burden all citizens must shoulder. Discrimination against people with disabilities compounds the difficulty of reintegrating injury victims into the social mainstream. In the most extreme cases, when the consequences of injuries become too great to bear, injury victims join the armies of the destitute that present our society with some of its most troubling challenges.

The creation of an impoverished and dependent social group can test the moral fiber of any society. We are all diminished by a social and legal system in which so many wrongful injuries are inflicted with impunity. We must consider whether it is acceptable that most injurers will never be held responsible, even when they're in the wrong, and that they will remain free to continue their risk-creating activities. Is it appropriate that they should be able to write off the slight chance of liability as a cost of doing business? The potential blow to our ideals must also be reckoned as part of the price we pay for the predominance of injuries without remedies.

Surely it is unfair and counterproductive to characterize the victims as malingerers, opportunists, and freeloaders. These are, after all, the *victims*. They are generally people of lesser means whose struggles have been made infinitely more difficult by harms others have inflicted. Yet most discussions of tort law, which is the primary mechanism for recourse the American legal system provides, are tilted against them. It is time to start again, armed with the recognition that injury victims are not a litigious lot but are loathe to make any sort of claim against their injurers. The problem is not too many claims but too few solutions.

EXISTING WORK-AROUNDS

"Work-around": a plan or method to circumvent a problem (as in computer software) without eliminating it.
Merriam-Webster's Dictionary

Although tort law judges, lawyers, and theorists have generally failed to appreciate the magnitude of lumping in

American society, they have developed some mechanisms to increase access to the courts or otherwise address the injury problem, even when injury victims lack the will or the resources to pursue their claims. We might view these mechanisms as "work-arounds" for the missing plaintiff problem. They have the capacity to retain some of the benefits tort law aims to achieve—though each of them has weaknesses or drawbacks. Before concluding with a more global recommendation, I will briefly remind readers of these already existing patches for the system, as well as their problems and potential.

1. Increasing Access to Lawyers

After lawyers were first permitted to advertise their services in the 1970s, personal injury specialists soon recognized that mass advertising would allow them to dip into the large, untapped market of injury victims who don't claim. A new form of high-volume, high-settlement practice emerged, which has encouraged some injury victims to abandon lumping and consider suing. Nora Freeman Engstrom calls these law firms "settlement mills,"[5] and highlights both their positive and negative features. The positives are actually considerable. Injury victims who never knew they might have a valid claim or didn't know how to approach an attorney are now more likely to make a phone call or send a text message and seek a remedy. Compensation from the injurer is now available to far more victims than it was under the more traditional forms of personal injury practice. Even those with small claims now have an opportunity to recover damages from their injurer.

But the drawbacks of this high-volume, mass-advertising approach are also substantial. They include a lack of individualized attention to the clients, overreliance on nonprofessionals to screen and evaluate cases, and preference by the attorneys for a quick and modest settlement over individualized, zealous advocacy case by case. Many lawyers and laypeople are troubled by the vulgarity of the commercials, whose poor taste and lack of professionalism make attorneys seem like used-car sellers. The public's low opinion of tort law in general certainly owes a great deal to these irritating advertisements. Public opinion does matter, not only because negative perceptions of tort law discourage injury victims from coming forward but also because they tend to instill an antiplaintiff bias among potential jurors in personal injury cases. In this sense, the more offensive commercials for personal injury lawyers play into the hands of the tort reformers' message about personal injury law as a haven for socially marginal claimants and unscrupulous attorneys. Unless this problem can be corrected, mass advertising may undermine the legitimacy of the tort law system even as it extends its reach into the silent legions of injury victims.

2. High Profile Impact Cases

Although most injury victims do not lodge claims of any kind, some of tort law's goals can be achieved when lawyers bring a few carefully chosen lawsuits with a particularly visible impact. Such lawsuits can publicize and correct serious injury problems and bring compensation to at least some of the victims— while encouraging settlements for others who don't simply lump. The recent history of tort law offers many examples of important impact litigation. In the late 1970s, Richard Grimshaw sued the Ford Motor Company for severe burns suffered when his Pinto exploded in flames after being rear-ended. Although Grimshaw's record-breaking award of $127,841,000 was reduced after the trial to "only" $3.5 million,[6] his lawsuit was considered one of the most notable of its era. It contributed not just to other Pinto claims and to safety regulations concerning rear-end collisions, but also to industry-wide safety practices and recall procedures that are still in effect today. Similarly, after Rose Cipollone died of lung cancer, her family sued the Liggett Group, makers of Cipollone's cigarettes, and a trial jury for the first time held a tobacco manufacturer liable for selling cigarettes. The United States Supreme Court affirmed the decision in 1992, and the legal protections previously enjoyed by tobacco companies began to crumble.[7] This trailblazing tort action changed the face of American tobacco sales and advertising and has surely prevented thousands of deaths and illnesses from cigarette smoking.

Cases like these are "work-arounds" for the problem of the reluctant plaintiff, since they don't depend on all or most injury victims coming forward. They require only a few representative victims whose claims are particularly likely to succeed. Lawyers around the country sometimes cooperate on strategies and choose the plaintiffs whose circumstances make success most probable. Impact litigation is well suited to serve tort law's historic deterrent function, but its weakness is its inability to provide compensation for all the similarly situated injury victims who are not parties to the lawsuit. Although in theory a successful high profile case should establish a framework for settlements by other injury victims, in practice we know that most victims will never reach the stage of claiming where settlement negotiations might take place. Thus, impact litigation achieves some but not all of the professed goals of tort law, despite its capacity to change dangerous social practices and reduce risks to the public at large.

3. Aggregating Claims

Another solution to the problem of the reluctant plaintiff is claim aggregation. When large numbers of plaintiffs can combine their claims, relatively inactive plaintiffs are able to ride the coattails of the more active parties and reap at least some of the rewards of a successful lawsuit.

One of the best-known forms of claim aggregation is the class action. In 1966, revisions of Rule 23 of the Federal Rules of Civil Procedure made it much more feasible to consolidate a number of similar legal claims against identical defendants into a single "class action" lawsuit. These changes did benefit some personal injury victims and led to well-publicized settlements in cases involving extremely harmful products, such as Agent Orange, Dalkon Shield, asbestos, and lead-based paint. Today, however, it's doubtful that any of those groups of plaintiffs could be certified as a class under Rule 23. Over time, the initial expansive vision for class actions was narrowed by judicial interpretation and legislative modification.[8] Howard M. Erichson notes that the drafters in 1966 had cautioned from the beginning against the use of class actions for mass torts. Despite an "upward trend" in the late 1980s and early 1990s, courts then "squelched that development" at the federal level, and only in state courts have personal injury lawyers had even mixed success using the class action mechanism.[9] Although some experts believe that the more draconian restrictions on class action plaintiffs can be reversed, the use of class actions by personal injury victims was always in doubt and will remain questionable even if the predicted "end of class actions"[10] can be averted.

Personal injury cases, with a few notable exceptions, seem ill-suited to the procedural requirements of the class action suit. The most numerous types of injuries in American society—including falls, negligent driving, intentional harms, and medical errors—involve different potential defendants for each plaintiff, as well as highly individualized circumstances and harms.[11] It's not surprising that these dissimilar injuries and unrelated injury claims resist the kind of consolidation offered by the class action suit.

Discussion of aggregating claims should not, however, be

confined to class actions. Samuel Issacharoff and John Fabian Witt suggest that, despite the seemingly individualized character of tort claims, aggregation has typified injury settlements throughout American history. They point out that claim aggregation isn't confined to "official" mechanisms and procedures, such as class actions, multidistrict consolidation, bankruptcy proceedings, and victim compensation funds, but also a variety of "unofficial" practices that develop over time. Issacharoff and Witt show that plaintiff and defense lawyers and insurance companies have always found it expedient to group large numbers of claims and settle them en masse rather then expending the time and money to consider each of them on the merits or—worst case—to litigate them separately.[12] Issacharoff and Witt's discussion of aggregation in automobile claims is especially noteworthy, since negligent driving remains one of the more frequent causes of injury in America. In these cases, highly routinized settlement practices by insurers tend to match the emergence of repeat-player plaintiffs' attorneys, resulting in "package deals" that can quickly resolve large numbers of claims in a single negotiation.[13]

Issacharoff and Witt consider this sort of aggregation in the tort field "inevitable." It allows for the faster and more efficient compensation of injury victims, and it provides payment to many whose claims might be too weak or too small to merit individualized attention. Of course, aggregation carries serious risks, as well. Strong claims can be "averaged down" to amounts smaller than the claimant would receive on an individual basis. Aggregate settlements may cover up the most egregious and risky practices of injurers and take out of play the punitive sanctions that would adequately deter them. Moreover, representatives of the plaintiffs and defendants may engage in trade-offs to strengthen their long-term bargaining relationship but disadvantage the short-term interests of individual injury victims.

The ultimate form of claim aggregation was adopted more than forty years ago in New Zealand, which eliminated tort law entirely and replaced it with a government-administered accident compensation scheme.[14] That is a strategy Americans would almost certainly reject on political grounds. But other forms of claim aggregation are already commonplace in our society and represent at least a partial work-around for the problem of the reluctant plaintiff.

4. Regulation

Regulation represents another existing work-around for the problem of the missing injury plaintiff, although it operates outside the tort system itself. Enforcement of safety standards or practices tends to reinforce the policy goal of deterrence, sometimes very effectively. Regulation deters injuries ex ante rather than ex post. Tort law is backward looking. It waits for injuries to occur and then, when called upon, does something about them.[15] Regulation is forward looking. It anticipates injuries and nips them in the bud.

Without question, many injuries and deaths in our society are prevented every year by the activities of government agencies. Safety standards issued by the National Highway Traffic Safety Administration have made motor vehicles far safer than in the past. Testing and approval of new prescription drugs and medical devices by the Food and Drug Administration has provided assurance of safe and effective products. The Consumer Product Safety Commission issues regulations, mandatory standards, and bans as well as monitoring voluntary safety standards for consumer products. The Occupational Safety and Health Administration makes the workplace safer and healthier by issuing and enforcing standards as well as providing training and education. These are just a few examples of federal government agencies that deter injuries, and countless others perform similar functions at the state level.

Unfortunately, regulation has its shortcomings as a mechanism to deal with injuries. Regulation's strong suit is prevention, but its weak suit is compensation. Once an injury occurs, regulatory agencies have only a limited capacity to improve the lives of the victims. Moreover, since tort actions often inspire new regulatory activity, injury victims' avoidance of litigation also tends to suppress regulation. Regulatory agencies are incapable of identifying or anticipating every new risk ahead of time. The regulatory net will always have gaps, and regulation tends to lag behind rapidly changing social and technological changes. Regulatory agencies are not as nimble and easily mobilized as individual claimants. They lack the capacity and often the political will to act against powerful organizations associated with harmful behavior. Political leaders and legislators may attempt to limit the activities of regulatory agencies and can reduce their budgets and staffs if they wish to rein them in. Regulatory agencies are notoriously prone to industry capture and to undue influence on their activities resulting from the "revolving door" careers of the regulators in the very industries they purport to control.

In this divisive and conservative political era, we must be realistic in our expectations about the prospects for vigorous regulatory activity unless private tort law plaintiffs provide an equally vigorous boost. For all the reasons addressed in this book, it seems unlikely that injury victims as a group will contribute the stimulus required for an expanded role of government regulatory agencies. Furthermore, it is ironic that the same voices calling for less tort law also call for less regulation. They do not view regulation as a desirable alternative or work-around to be promoted in place of personal injury litigation but as another form of meddlesome and costly intervention with private industry and the market.

It should be noted, however, that regulation need not come from the government. Industries and professions often self-regulate by instituting their own safety standards and disciplinary procedures. Trans-industry organizations, such as the American National Standards Institute (ANSI), can also be a powerful force for injury reduction. Thus, regulation in all of its varied forms does represent a significant mechanism for dealing with our society's injury problem. Although regulation is often activated by individual injury claimants, it doesn't passively await claims in the same way that tort law does, and to this extent it represents a partial work-around for the predominance of lumping among injury victims.

THE CASE FOR CULTURE CHANGE

For last year's words belong to last year's language
And next year's words await another voice.
T. S. Eliot, "Little Gidding"[16]

My aim in writing this book was not to solve the injury problem in American society or to "fix" our tort law system. Rather, I have argued that it is essential to reframe the questions we ask and bring to our policy debates a recognition that most injury victims do not lodge claims against their injurers. In short, we need to go beyond the discourse that now prevails when discussing injuries and the law. We need to find another voice that is more true to the experiences of injury victims and better able to express the issues injuries pose for them and for society as a whole.

What might such a discussion look like, and where would it lead us? For one thing, a responsible public debate about injuries would be evidence based. Surely we have no more need for social policy based on fiction, misleading anecdotes, deliberate distortion, and misperception. In the policy debates to come, we should ground our positions on the substantial body of research dealing with injuries, injury victims, and the role law actually plays. It is entirely possible to acknowledge the real facts about lumping and claiming and still disagree respectfully about how to solve the injury problem in our society. Fact-based disagreement is preferable to fantasy-based consensus.

In this new conversation, if the participants frankly acknowledge the predominance of lumping among injury victims, the "work-arounds" discussed in the preceding section will take on a heightened significance. Yet we've also seen that none of the work-arounds can, in itself, achieve what tort law purports to provide—compensation *and* deterrence, loss distribution *and* corrective justice. Perhaps no single mechanism or institution can do all of these things. But we can't simply abandon these policy goals, even if the data suggest that tort law alone is incapable of achieving them. Some combination of improved access to attorneys, claim aggregation, impact litigation, and regulation may, in an imperfect world, move us a little closer to realizing our aspirations as a society.

As I consider the lessons learned from writing this book, one policy response seems more promising than any other. If I were granted only one wish to improve our public debate and bring greater clarity and rationality to this turbulent field, it would be this: We have experienced a significant cultural shift over the past few decades, affecting the way most Americans view injuries. It has instilled a mostly negative and often unsympathetic view of injury victims and their lawyers. This shift was no accident. It was the result of careful planning, political strategizing, and targeted funding. I would seek to challenge and transform this new cultural consensus and replace it with a more balanced, humane, nuanced, and respectful framework for understanding injuries, injurers, and injury victims. The result would not necessarily be more (or fewer) injury claims, but rather a heightened sense that we as a collectivity must somehow address the need to prevent injuries, achieve fairness, and protect victims from devastating financial and personal losses. Even those who oppose tort law should feel obliged to explain how they would achieve these fundamental goals.

For a law professor to conclude by proposing a strategy of culture change rather than a specific legal reform may seem surprising. Legal books and articles typically end with a model statute, a recommendation to judges for deciding future cases, or a new regulatory scheme. But lawyers very often overestimate the power of law to accomplish social change. They try—sometimes in vain—to construct tails strong enough to wag a very large dog. Stewart Macaulay used to ask provocatively which event contributed more to the advancement of racial equality: the landmark school integration decision of the United States Supreme Court in *Brown v. Board of Education* or Jackie Robinson joining the Brooklyn Dodgers.

Macaulay's question may be difficult to answer, but it's quite easy to identify the single event that has had the biggest impact on the practice and perception of modern American tort law—and that is the McDonald's hot coffee case. Stella Liebeck's lawsuit led to a minor legal victory for the plaintiff but a major cultural triumph for defendants everywhere. Never has losing felt so much like winning! No development in the law of torts has affected more injury victims, lawyers, and jurors than the mythologizing of Stella Liebeck's misfortune and modest settlement into a misleading story that was heard and believed around the world. The McDonald's coffee narrative has shaped American tort law more profoundly than any statute or judicial decision.

This book has demonstrated why the myth of the McDonald's case had such an extraordinary impact. The social and cultural environment plays a crucial role in shaping public viewpoints toward injuries as well as the behavior of victims and injurers. Lumping and claiming take place within a particular social and cultural setting. To the extent that American culture is imbued with negative imagery of tort law, plaintiffs, and their lawyers, it shapes behavior from the moment an injury occurs until the relatively rare moment when a claim is actually litigated. Personal injury attorneys enter the courtroom knowing that jurors—who are immersed in the same social and cultural environment—are suspicious of their clients and deeply skeptical about their motives.

The McDonald's case illustrates the extraordinary power of a "culture change" strategy. But cultures are human constructs. What has been constructed can be deconstructed and reconstructed. "Last year's language" can be replaced by "next year's words" and "another voice." If cultures are indeed webs of meaning that humans themselves have spun,[17] then we can spin new webs and create new meanings. We can tell different stories about injury victims and portray them as ordinary people—like you and me—who suffered terrible, life-changing setbacks at the hands of another person. When risk-creating activities are excessive or unreasonable, they should be seen for what they are, as unfair attempts by the injurers to shift responsibility and costs from themselves to the victims. Such practices represent threats to all of us. A new narrative would not single out the victims for blame but would emphasize that we are all potential victims.

If we are to make a new beginning in the public debates over injury and the law, both narratives should be equally available and familiar—the narrative of self-sufficiency *and* the narrative of social responsibility. Both are associated with legitimate and persuasive policy positions, and they are often in conflict with one another. There is nothing wrong with conflict-ing perspectives on important questions. But it is impossible to have a reasonable discussion about social policy when one of these narratives about injury and injury victims has totally van-quished and silenced the other with a barrage of misinforma-tion. That is currently the situation, and it should be changed.

How might a culture change strategy be pursued? The suc-cess of the tort reform movement in the 1980s and 1990s pro-vides a useful roadmap. It demonstrates the value of investing effort and money in public relations. Targeted advertisements in the mass media have had a pervasive impact and could be used just as effectively to communicate the proposed counter-narrative. In addition, Hollywood has proved receptive to por-traying the victims' perspective in some situations. Films such as *Erin Brockovich, A Civil Action,* and *The Rainmaker* por-trayed personal injury plaintiffs and lawyers in a more positive light and made the social problem of injury understandable to a wide audience, despite the usual cinematic exaggerations. In addition, documentaries such as the recent film *Hot Coffee,* which countered the tort reformers' version of the McDonald's story, can balance public perceptions by introducing a criti-cal examination of corporate policies. A culture change strat-egy would demonstrate that there really are two sides to many of these issues and would replace dismissive attitudes with a more thoughtful appreciation of the different interests at stake.

Of course, high profile injury litigation should continue in worthy causes. Such litigation can also generate publicity that is more sympathetic to the plight of injury victims. But, on the whole, mass media reporting of tort law has failed to convey the plaintiffs' position and has tended to support the tort re-formers' message of individual responsibility rather than giv-ing equal time to the social obligations of injurers.[18] A culture change strategy would attempt to reverse this tendency by print and broadcast media so that the positions of both sides—injurers and victims—receive fair exposure. If media reporting could be focused more consistently on the most widespread and costly injuries in American society, and if it could identify new risks through investigative journalism and exposés, that in itself would contribute significantly to injury reduction. Individuals could guard against the dangers that were reported; markets could respond to the riskiest products and services; and government regulators could take note and concentrate their efforts on the injuries that received this public exposure. In short, no legal strategy imaginable would have the impact of a cultural shift that, instead of demonizing injury victims and their attorneys, portrayed their interests as fully and respectfully as those of their injurers.

A cultural shift of this kind would also make visible some of the irrational and counterproductive results of tort reform legislation enacted by many states. For example, caps on non-economic damage awards and on punitive damages have done nothing to solve a real problem—the fact that small injury claims tend to be overcompensated—but have made much worse the well-documented tendency to undercompensate large claims.[19] There is credible evidence that tort reform restrictions have fallen disproportionately on the most vulnerable and needful plaintiffs—women, the elderly, the unemployed, and the poor—and left many of them without representation or access to justice.[20]

Almost by definition, tort reform measures have done nothing to address widespread lumping by injury victims. Indeed, the reformers have denied the very existence of the phenomenon and have contended that the tiny percentage of injury victims who do litigate is far too large. There is very little empirical evidence that tort reform has achieved any of the results touted by its proponents. It's true that tort litigation rates have gone down. But lowering the number of lawsuits should not be an end in itself. Good policy would aim to reduce only frivolous lawsuits while ensuring that those with merit succeed in our justice system. There is no evidence that the reduction in tort cases has resulted from screening out only the unreasonable or unfair claims. Moreover, the supposed social benefits of tort reform, including reductions in insurance rates, lower costs of goods and services, or improved supply of doctors, have not been demonstrated empirically.[21] Meanwhile, the problem of lumping has gone unaddressed and has certainly gotten worse. Tort reform has had the cynical and perverse effect of making lumping even more attractive rather than reducing injuries or improving the lives of injury victims.

If we were to initiate a new beginning, replacing last year's language with a new and more responsible discussion of injuries and the law, the most harmful effects of tort reform would be exposed as we move ahead collectively to determine how best to address the real problems of injury in our society.

CONCLUDING THOUGHTS

The purpose of this book is to refocus attention on injury victims and the law. It has attempted to ask a counterintuitive question—why most injury victims settle for lumping even when they may have been wronged by someone else. It has provided a set of answers that portray victims and injurers in a new light. The phenomenon that demands explanation is not why tort law is used so often but why so many injury victims make no claim at all despite their sometimes desperate circumstances. I argue that the cloud of rhetoric surrounding tort law, and the false and misleading claims of self-interested parties, has obscured our understanding of injuries in American society—what they really are, how they affect all of us, how most people respond, what we can do to promote safety, and how we can make sure that those who suffer harm do not experience personal devastation as a result.

It is unfortunate that political agendas have overwhelmed the needed conversation about these crucially important questions. The issues are essentially human. Different political and social philosophies may generate different responses—and that is entirely fair and appropriate. But the public debate should center on real questions and should be informed by real facts, not bizarre and demeaning fantasies. Such a conversation will be possible if there is a better understanding of how people actually respond to injuries in our society—and why. In presenting the most reliable and pertinent data concerning the lives, perceptions, and decisions of injury victims, I join those who have called for a more responsible debate about where we need to go next. That would be a discussion worth having.

ACKNOWLEDGMENTS

〜〜

This book originated in a series of conversations with John Tryneski, executive editor at the University of Chicago Press. John's encouragement, advice, and friendship were invaluable from beginning to end. Like many law and society scholars, I am deeply in his debt, as is our field in general.

I benefited from the suggestions and critiques of numerous colleagues, many of whom read part or all of the manuscript. Those who deserve special thanks include Dianne Avery, Lynette Chua, Tom Baker, Samantha Barbas, Christine Bartholomew, Anya Bernstein, Anne Bloom, Anya Engel, Fred Konefsky, Lynn Mather, Michael McCann, Frank Munger, and Barbara Yngvesson. The topic of the book grew out of a presentation at a conference organized by Stephan Landsman at DePaul Law School to honor the work of Marc Galanter. Marc and his writings on the United States and India have been a source of inspiration for many years.

Readers familiar with the law and society field will recognize how extensively I have drawn on its theories and its research literature in formulating my arguments. I am grateful to the many friends and colleagues in the Law & Society Association whose work has contributed so profoundly to my understanding of this topic.

I wish to thank five hardworking research assistants, all current or former students at SUNY Buffalo Law School: Frances Helen Stephenson, Lauren Gray, Greg Bonney, Christine Sullivan, and Nara Tjitradjaja. They will recognize their many contributions on nearly every page of this book.

My family was, as ever, encouraging, supportive, and patient with their preoccupied husband/father. Thanks to Jaruwan, Anya, Mark, and Patrick for reminding me always of what's most important.

NOTES

CHAPTER ONE

1. The complete expression appears in various forms. One of the most common is "It ain't what you don't know that gets you into trouble. It's what you know for sure that just ain't so." Though often attributed to Mark Twain, and sometimes to Will Rogers and even Josh Billings (Henry Wheeler Shaw), the quote's origin remains uncertain.

2. Doyle 1930 at 347.

3. See National Safety Council 2014.

4. The quotation may be apocryphal. It is sometimes said to appear in his novel *The House of the Dead* (1862), but commentators do not provide a precise citation, and a close reading of the novel yields no passage even approximately like this.

5. Cohen and Harbacek 2011, table 5, at 4 (based on a national sample taken from urban, suburban, and rural jurisdictions).

6. Rabin 2012 at 3.

7. Medical Injury Compensation Reform Act 1975.

8. Jury awards in medical malpractice cases after MICRA dropped by 25 percent in nonfatal injuries and 51 percent in cases involving fatalities. Awards to females dropped by a median amount of 34 percent compared to a 25 percent drop for males. Pace, Golinelli, and Zakaras 2004 at xx–xxiii. See also Devito and Jurs 2014 at 555.

9. Baker 2005.

10. Zollers, Hurd, and Shears 2000; Henderson and Eisenberg 1990.

11. Schwartz 1992; Henderson and Eisenberg 1990 at 481.

12. Haltom and McCann 2004 at 40–45.

13. McGarity 2013 at 207.

14. See Haltom and McCann 2004.

15. Nockleby and Curreri 2005 at 1021.

16. Daniels and Martin 2000 at 473–74.

17. See, e.g., Kritzer, Bogart, and Vidmar 1991 at 505; Saks 1992 at 1183–85; Genn 1999 at 9; Murayama 2007 at 31; Engel and Engel 2010 at 79–80 and 159–61.

18. Friedman 1985 at 5.

CHAPTER TWO

1. *Webster's Unabridged Dictionary of the English Language* 2001, s.v. "lumping."

2. Felstiner 1974 at 81.

3. See Stewart, Cohen, and Marangi 2002 at 153–78; Ackerman 2005 at 135–229; Fein and Alexander 2003 at 692–718.

4. Hensler et al. 1991 at 8.

5. Hensler et al. 1991 at 109n.

6. Hensler et al. 1991, table 5.5, at 125.

7. Hensler et al. 1991, table 5.6, at 127.

8. Abel 1987 at 448–52.

9. Abel 1987 at 452.

10. Baker 2005 at 70.

11. See Miller and Sarat 1980–81.

12. *Grimshaw v. Ford Motor Co.* 1981.

13. Saks 1992. Saks drew on three databases in which medical experts had made prior determinations of the presence or absence of medical error: (1) a study by what was then the U.S. Department of Health, Education, and Welfare in 1972; (2) a joint study by the California Hospital Association and the California Medical Association published in 1977; and (3) a 1990 study by researchers at the Harvard School of Public Health focused on New York hospital discharges.

14. Galanter 1983 at 14.

15. Haltom and McCann 2004 at 81.

16. Saks 1992 at 1287.

17. For examples of comparative studies of injury disputes in other countries, see FitzGerald 1983 (Australia); Kritzer, Bogart, and Vidmar 1991 (Canada); Blankenburg 1994 (Western Europe); Genn 1999 (England and Wales); Genn and Paterson 2001 (Scotland).

18. Murayama 2007 at 29.

19. Felstiner, Abel, and Sarat 1980–81.

20. Galanter 1996.

21. See, e.g., Miller and Sarat 1980–81 at 544; FitzGerald 1983 at 29; Galanter 1996 at 1099–1100; Burris et al. 2000 at 239, 242; Murayama 2007 at 29, 30; Michelson 2007 at 467.

CHAPTER THREE

1. Daudet 2002 [1930] at 31.

2. Greenberg 2009 at 42–43.

3. Heshusius 2009 at 15.

4. Bendelow and Williams 1995 at 87.

5. Wilde 2003 at 170.

6. Bendelow and Williams 1995 at 88.

7. Jackson 2011 at 381.

8. See Csordas 2011 at 149–50.

9. See Jackson 2011 at 381 ("Some accounts vividly describe rejection, in no uncertain terms, of the painful body part."). See also de Vignemont 2011.

10. See Carpenter 1994 at 621 ("It took at least 4 years before things began to click into place, and life goes on fairly normally.").

11. Carpenter 1994 at 623 (quoting an interviewee identified by the pseudonym "Randy") (emphasis added).

12. See Lucas 2003, table 1, at 137–38. Another study reported "immediate anxiety" as a significant response to pain. See Crockett, Prkachin, and Craig 1977–78 at 179.

13. Lucas 2003 at 142. According to Lucas, women appeared to be particularly susceptible to these symptoms.

14. Greenberg 2009 at 48.

15. Heshusius 2009 at 88–89.

16. Greenberg 2009 at 68.

17. Goffman 1963 at 6.

18. Goffman 1963 at 12.

19. Heshusius 2009 at 17.

20. Scarry 1985 at 4.

21. Jackson 1994 at 222.

22. Heshusius 2009 at 15.

23. Greenberg 2009 at 46–48. Greenberg notes that it later became apparent to her that the pain medication as well as the pain itself contributed to her loss of language.

24. Jackson 2011 at 378.

25. See, e.g., Wright 1983 at 64 (explaining that persons without disabilities unconsciously believe that "the cripple has committed some evil act"); Cook 2004 at 462 (noting a common perception that injuries are part of God's plan, except when the defendant clearly sinned by choosing to disobey God).

26. Bendelow and Williams 1995 at 92.

27. Johansson et al. 1999 at 1795.

28. Schulz and Decker 1985 at 1166.

CHAPTER FOUR

1. Watson 2011.

2. Csordas 1994 at 9.

3. Kahneman 2011 at 51 (emphasis added).

4. Johnson 2007 at 145.

5. Davis and Markman 2012 at 690.

6. Damasio 2012 at 22.

7. Damasio 2012 at 215.

8. Damasio 2012 at 24.

9. Damasio 2012 at 223–24.

10. Damasio 2012 at 223.

11. Thaler and Sunstein 2008 at 6–8.

12. Thaler and Sunstein 2008 at 7–8.

13. Damasio 2012 at 23–26.

14. Kahneman 2011 at 21–22.

15. Kahneman 2011 at 71.

16. Bargh 1997 at 50.

17. Haidt 2012 at 45–46.

18. Williams and Bargh 2008 at 606–7. Discussed in Glenberg 2010 at 586–96.

19. Barsalou 2008 at 630.

20. Kahneman 2011 at 411.

21. See Kelman 2011 at 229–30.

22. Kahneman 2011 at 63–66.

23. Kahneman 2011 at 87–88.

24. See Thaler and Sunstein 2008 at 5–6.

25. "[S]tatus quo framing was found to have predictable and significant effects on subjects' decision making." Samuelson and Zeckhauser 1988 at 8.

26. Samuelson and Zeckhauser 1988 at 39–40.

CHAPTER FIVE

1. This aphorism has been widely quoted and is usually attributed to Garret FitzGerald. See Cowell 2011.

2. Mencken 1919 at 5.

3. See Stinchcombe 1968 at 5.

4. Kahneman 2011 at 81.

5. Doyle 1930 at 163 (from "A Scandal in Bohemia").

6. Manning 1977 coined the term "hyperlexis" in a widely cited article entitled "Hyperlexis: Our National Disease."

7. Lave and March 1993 at 19.

8. "[Pain] is unequivocally a complex perceptual process that originates in the brain. . . . In the formation of the perception that we recognize as pain, the brain inextricably intertwines sensory information with emotions and cognition." Chapman 1995 at 284.

9. Lakoff and Johnson 1999 at 517–18.

10. Lave and March 1993 at 108.

11. Johnson 2007 at 276.

12. Johnson 2007 at 276.

13. Merleau-Ponty 1958 at 499–500.

14. Bruner 1990 at 114.

CHAPTER SIX

1. See tylervigen.com (accessed September 4, 2015).

2. Hume 1999.

3. Lakoff and Johnson 1999 at 230–31 (italics in original deleted).

4. Lakoff and Johnson 1999 at 187.

5. Lakoff and Johnson 1999 at 231.

6. See Franklin and Nelson 2003 at 1032–34. See also National Multiple Sclerosis Society, n.d.

7. Voltaire 1919 at 232.

8. Coates and Penrod 1980–81 at 665.

9. Nadler 2012 at 9.

10. Malone 1956 at 62.

11. See Lakoff and Johnson 1999 at 13.

12. Bergstrom 1992 at 173.

13. Bergstrom 1992 at 168.

14. Engel 1984.

15. Cook 2004 at 462.

16. Wenner 2003.

17. *New York Central Railroad v. Grimstad* 1920.

18. *New York Central Railroad v. Grimstad* 1920 at 335.

19. This sort of counterfactual reasoning is typical of tort law's approach to the proof of causation. The "but for" test requires the finder of fact to determine whether, absent the defendant's wrongful act, the plaintiff would have been injured anyway. Causation is established only if the plaintiff can prove by a preponderance of the evidence that, *but for* the negligent act, plaintiff would not have suffered the harm that occurred. Thus, each causal inquiry begins by hypothesizing an imaginary world free from defendant's misconduct and then asking what plaintiff's fate would have been in that world.

20. *Zinnel v. U.S. Shipping Board Emergency Fleet Corporation* 1925.

21. See Hovenkamp 1982.

22. See Galanter 1974.

23. Hensler et al. 1991, table 3.18, at 49.

24. Coates and Penrod 1980–81 at 666.

CHAPTER SEVEN

1. *Montesinos v. Daly* 2009. See also saintpatrickscathedral.org (accessed September 4, 2015).

2. National Safety Council 2014 at 20 and 168; Cohen 2000 at 11–12; Pauls 1991 at 130.

3. The RAND Corporation study found that, when hurt in accidents not involving motor vehicles or on-the-job product-associated accidents, only 1 percent of injury victims hired lawyers. No figures were provided specifically for stairway accidents, but it is reasonable to assume that the involvement of lawyers in such accidents would not differ greatly from similar accident types cited in the RAND study. Of the 1 percent who hired lawyers, an unspecified but certainly smaller fraction eventually filed lawsuits. See Hensler et al. 1991 at 124.

4. See Jackson and Cohen 1995 at 153.

5. Jackson and Cohen 1995 at 156.

6. See Jackson and Cohen 1995 at 156–58: "We believe from examining our data and the literature that the strongest pattern for stairway accidents lies in dimensional inconsistency within stairways."

7. Cohen 2009 at 32.

8. "Defendants have established that none of the codes generally, or code sections specifically, are controlling. St. Patrick's Cathedral was built well before the New York City Building Code came into effect, and therefore is not subject to its provisions under the grandfathering clause of Administrative Code § 27-111." *Montesinos v. Daly* 2009 at 10.

9. Cranz 1998.

10. Cranz 1998 at 56.

11. Buckley et al. 2013 at 109–11.

12. Cranz 1998 at 101–2.

13. Cranz 1998 at 105.

14. Levine 2014 at 34–35.

15. www.getbritainstanding.org (accessed September 4, 2015).

16. Jain 2006 at 86. See also Amell and Kumar 1999 at 69–78.

17. Jain 2006 at 97.

18. Jain 2006 at 109. See also Noyes 1983.

19. Amell and Kumar 1999 at 72.

20. Dvorak 1943.

21. Jain 2006 at 191n323.

22. *Dreisonstok v. Volkswagenwerk* 1974 (holding that the design of the microbus was not defective because the risks associated with its unique profile should

not be compared to those of a vehicle with a hood that affords front-end crush space).

23. For a discussion of the cultural shifts associated with safety standards addressing the "second collision" in automobiles, see MacLennan 1988.

24. Radnofsky 2007.

25. Office of Regulatory Analysis and Evaluation, National Center for Statistics and Analysis 2014.

26. Hurwitz et al. 2010 at 79.

27. According to Hurwitz et al., 88 percent of the crashes under experimental conditions were prevented when drivers were attentive to the rearview cameras. The problem remained, however, that drivers in their experiments looked at the cameras only 20 percent of the time when backing up. See Hurwitz et al. 2010 at 83.

28. Hurwitz et al. found that 46 percent of the drivers who did not otherwise look at the rearview cameras while backing up would do so in response to an audible warning. See Hurwitz et al. 2010 at 83. Presumably, once these additional drivers looked at the camera, they experienced the same 88 percent rate of accident avoidance as the drivers that looked at the camera without any prompting.

29. Department of Transportation, National Highway Traffic Safety Administration, 49 CFR Part 571, Docket No. NHTSA-2010-0162, RIN 2127-AK43.

30. Lienert 2013.

31. For a comprehensive overview of the McDonald's hot coffee case as portrayed by popular media, see Haltom and McCann 2004 at 183–226.

32. See Haltom and McCann 2004 at 186: "Third-degree burns are extreme injuries in that they penetrate through the full thickness of the skin to the fat, muscle, and bone."

33. Haltom and McCann 2004 at 189–90.

34. See Haltom and McCann 2004 at 189–90.

35. Jain 2006 at 151.

36. Jain 2006 at 56.

37. Jain 2006 at 152.

CHAPTER EIGHT

1. Wallace 2009 at 3.

2. "Believing, with Max Weber, that man is an animal suspended in webs of significance he himself has spun, I take culture to be those webs. . . ." Geertz 1973 at 5.

3. *Merriam-Webster Online*, s.v. "injury" (accessed September 4, 2015).

4. Free 2002 at 143.

5. Jackson 2011 at 374.

6. Jackson 2011 at 372 (citing Beecher 1946).

7. See Engel 1984 at 558 (noting that farmers in "Sander County" recounted many serious injuries caused by dangers associated with their way of life and that they believed "injuries were an ever-present possibility"). See also Kumar, Varghese, and Mohan 2000 (discussing the frequency and severity of agricultural injuries across societies and cultures, as well as the tendency to associate such injuries with the conduct of the workers rather than consider modification of their working conditions or equipment).

8. See Howe 2001.

9. See Dunbar and Sabry 2007 at 37; see also Sloan and Hsieh 1995 at 426, 431.

10. Chang 2003 at 4–5; see also Levy 1966 at 26. The "virtual crippling" caused by foot binding, which was initiated in early childhood, resulted in the physical confinement and seclusion of "upper-class ladies" and "rendered [them] immune from the social disease of conjugal infidelity." Levy 1966 at 30. See also Blake 1994.

11. See Wright 1983 at 11. Foot binding ended rapidly in China during the first decade of the twentieth century as a result of dramatic shifts in social and cultural norms, as well as legal prohibitions. See Mackie 1996 at 1001.

12. Weila 2012 at 703.

13. Waldeck 2003 at 469–70.

14. Waldeck 2003 at 474.

15. Rabin 2010 (citing figures presented at an International AIDS conference in Vienna by CDC researcher Charbel E. El Becheraoui).

16. Weila 2012 at 700–701.

17. Waldeck 2003 at 477.

18. Davis 2001 at 527–28 (quoting Berlin 1989).

19. Brigman 1984–85 at 337. For a discussion of the cultural meaning and practice of male circumcision, see Silverman 2004.

20. Hofvander 2002 at 630; Kepe 2010.

21. Fateh-Moghadam 2012.

22. Fox and Thomson 2009 at 196.

23. For example, in *Fishbeck v. State of North Dakota* 1997, the Court of Appeals for the Eighth Circuit dismissed for lack of standing a claim brought by the mother of a male infant who had been circumcised without her consent. The plaintiff had claimed that the prohibition of circumcision for females but not for males violated the equal protection clause. The North Dakota Supreme Court reached a similar conclusion in *Flatt ex rel. Flatt v. Kantak* 2004, a case brought

on behalf of the male infant by his guardians. In *Flatt*, the court held that the plaintiff lacked standing to challenge the North Dakota statute criminalizing female but not male circumcision. By comparison, in the case of *In re Marriage of Boldt* 2008, the Oregon Supreme Court considered a petition by a divorced mother who sought to prevent her ex-husband from having their twelve-year-old son circumcised. At that time, the father had custody of the boy. The court sidestepped the fundamental question whether male circumcision was an injury and instead ruled that the wishes of the boy himself must be ascertained and given weight.

24. Friedman 1990 at 4.

25. Friedman 1985 at 5 (emphasis in original).

26. Greenhouse, Yngvesson, and Engel 1994.

27. Greenhouse, Yngvesson, and Engel 1994 at 129.

28. Greenhouse, Yngvesson, and Engel 1994 at 35.

29. Hensler et al. 1991, table 3.18, at 49.

30. Haltom and McCann 2004.

31. Haltom and McCann 2004 at 46.

32. Haltom and McCann 2004 at 185–89.

33. Chamallas and Wriggins 2010 at 170–72. See also Haltom and McCann 2004 at 96; Finley 2004 at 1267–68.

34. See Chamallas and Wriggins 2010 at 170–82.

35. Some studies of sexual harassment in the workplace (not necessarily involving personal injuries) note that women who have been victimized by such misconduct may resist bringing a legal challenge for fear of blame, retaliation, and other negative repercussions. See, e.g., Hebert 2007 at 724–25; Brake and Grossman 2008.

36. Hebert 2007 at 724n69 and 727n85.

37. Engel 1984 at 568.

38. Geertz 1983 at 167 ("Like sailing, gardening, politics, and poetry, law and ethnography are crafts of place: they work by the light of local knowledge."). Arthur Kleinman makes a related point, relevant in particular to injury cognition, by emphasizing that those who study the perception and interpretation of pain must take into account the "local moral worlds" in which the body experiences it. See Kleinman 1992 at 170.

CHAPTER NINE

1. Chamallas and Wriggins 2010 at 113–17.

2. Nedelsky 2011 at 19.

3. Fineman 2008 at 9–10.

4. The names of people, places, and organizations in this account are pseudonyms.

5. In 1975-76, the annual litigation rate for personal injury cases was only 1.45 cases per thousand population. See Engel 1984 at 552n1; Engel 1983.

6. The term "quorum decision-making" is explained in Ward et al. 2008. As Tunstrøm et al. note, "The patterns exhibited by moving animal groups like flocks of birds and schools of fish are typical of self-organizing systems in which global structural and dynamical properties arise from local interactions between individuals." Tunstrøm et al. 2013 at 2.

7. See Damasio 2012 at 223-24.

8. Bruner 1990 at 113-14.

9. See Engel and Munger 2003 at 45 ("The ever-changing stories people tell themselves and others about who they are alternate with 'new living action.' That is, narratives of the self follow and explain past experiences, but they also *precede* new experiences in which individuals attempt to act out the selves they have narrated and the desires and aspirations associated with those selves. . . ."). On the topic of narrative, identity, and future action, see also Rosenwald 1992 at 274 ("New living action follows a new story partly as a way of catching the life up to the account of the life and partly to express what is missing from the story."). This chapter's discussion of narrative, legal claims, and distributed identity draws on my previous work with Frank W. Munger. I gratefully acknowledge this fruitful collaboration. Frank's astute ideas and insights are an integral part of the discussion I present here.

10. Hardin and Conley 2001 at 9. See also Echterhoff, Higgins, and Levine 2009.

11. Echterhoff, Higgins, and Levine 2009 at 500.

12. Hardin and Conley 2001 at 16.

13. See Bourdieu 1977 at 80-82 (each episode of "*interaction* and mutual adjustment" is not an isolated social event, but takes place in an environment that already possesses certain "objective structures which have produced the dispositions of the interacting agents.").

14. Pennington, Gillen, and Hill 1999 at 109.

15. Schank and Abelson 1977 at 41.

16. Jost, Ledgerwood, and Hardin 2008 at 174.

17. Jost, Ledgerwood, and Hardin 2008 at 181.

18. Pennington, Gillen, and Hill 1999 at 117.

19. Kahneman 2011 at 52-54.

20. Kahneman 2011 at 53 (citing an experiment by John Bargh and colleagues).

21. Gergen 1994 at 17.

22. Gergen 1994 at 66–67.

23. Kahneman 2011 at 129.

24. Haidt 2012 at 47.

25. See Hickson et al. 1992 at 1361 (noting that 33 percent of families that filed medical malpractice claims following perinatal injuries cited advice by knowledgeable acquaintances as a significant factor in their decision).

26. See Haltom and McCann 2004 at 28–29 (the mass media influence public opinion to favor the "individual responsibility" perspective toward injuries rather than one that would justify legal claims). See also Engel 1984 at 558–59 (noting the predominance in Sander County, Illinois, of a type of individualism that emphasizes self-sufficiency rather than rights and remedies in injury cases).

27. Kritzer 2004 at 72.

28. Kritzer 2004 at 84–86.

29. See Robbennolt 2003 at 484–88.

30. See Landro 2007.

31. Compare Lovallo and Kahneman 2003.

CHAPTER TEN

1. Mearns, n.d.

2. Ross 1980.

3. Saks 1992 at 1287.

4. Posner 1972 at 33.

5. Engstrom 2011.

6. *Grimshaw v. Ford Motor Company* 1981.

7. *Cipollone v. Liggett Group, Inc.* 1992. See also Mather 2009.

8. Miller 2014 at 297.

9. Erichson 2005 at 1772–73.

10. Fitzpatrick 2015.

11. According to Cohen 2009 at 2, the most common types of tort cases tried in state courts—where most tort actions are brought—were automobile accidents (58 percent), medical malpractice (15 percent), premises liability (11 percent), and intentional torts (4 percent).

12. Issacharoff and Witt 2004.

13. Issacharoff and Witt 2004 at 1614.

14. See Schuck 2008.

15. Sometimes tort law takes on a quasi-regulatory aspect, but it cannot be triggered until someone brings a claim.

16. Eliot 1952 at 141.

17. Geertz 1973 at 5.

18. Haltom and McCann 2004 at 147–81.

19. "This pattern of overcompensation at the lower end of the range and undercompensation at the higher end is so well replicated that it qualifies as one of the major empirical phenomena of tort litigation ready for theoretical attention." Saks 1992 at 1218.

20. Daniels and Martin 2000; Finley 2004.

21. Eisenberg 2013.

REFERENCES

BOOKS AND ARTICLES

Abel, Richard L. 1987. "The Real Tort Crisis—Too *Few* Claims." *Ohio State Law Journal* 48(2): 443-67.

Ackerman, Robert M. 2005. "The September 11th Victim Compensation Fund: An Effective Administrative Response to National Tragedy." *Harvard Negotiation Law Review* 10: 135-229.

Amell, T. K., and S. Kumar. 1999. "Cumulative Trauma Disorders and Keyboarding Work." *International Journal of Industrial Ergonomics* 25: 69-78.

Baker, Tom. 2005. *The Medical Malpractice Myth*. Chicago: University of Chicago Press.

Bargh, John A. 1997. "The Automaticity of Everyday Life." In *The Automaticity of Everyday Life: Advances in Social Cognition, Volume X*, edited by Robert S. Wyer Jr., 1-61. Mahwah, NJ: Lawrence Erlbaum Associates.

Barsalou, Lawrence W. 2008. "Grounded Cognition." *Annual Review of Psychology* 59: 617-45.

Beecher, Henry K. 1946. "Pain in Men Wounded in Battle." *Annals of Surgery* 123(1): 96-105.

Bendelow, Gillian, and Simon Williams. 1995. "Pain and the Mind-Body Dualism: A Sociological Approach." *Body & Society* 1(2): 87.

Bergstrom, Randolph E. 1992. *Courting Danger: Injury and Law in New York City, 1820-1910*. Ithaca, NY: Cornell University Press.

Berlin, Stuart M. 1989. "From the Jewish Journal: Don't Fear 'Brit Milah.'" *Berit Milah Newsletter* October 6, 1989 [as cited in Davis 2001 at 528].

Blake, C. Fred. 1994. "Foot-Binding in Neo-Confucian China and the Appropriation of Female Labor." *Signs* 19(3): 676-712.

Blankenburg, Erhard. 1994. "The Infrastructure for Avoiding Civil Litigation: Comparing Cultures of Legal Behavior in the Netherlands and West Germany." *Law & Society Review* 28(4): 789-808.

Bourdieu, Pierre. 1977. *Outline of a Theory of Practice*. Edited and translated by Richard Nice. Cambridge: Cambridge University Press.

Brake, Deborah L., and Joanna L. Grossman. 2008. "The Failure of Title VII as a Rights-Claiming System." *North Carolina Law Review* 86(4): 859-936.

Brigman, William E. 1984-85. "Circumcision as Child Abuse: The Legal and Constitutional Issues." *Journal of Family Law* 23(3): 337-57.

Bruner, Jerome. 1990. *Acts of Meaning*. Cambridge, MA: Harvard University Press.

Buckley, John P., Duane D. Mellor, Michael Morris, and Franklin Joseph. 2013. "Standing-Based Office Work Shows Encouraging Signs of Attenuating Post-Prandial Glycaemic Excursion." *Occupational and Environmental Medicine* 7: 109–11.

Burris, Scott, Kathryn Moss, Michael Darren Ullman, and Matthew Johnsen. 2000. "Disputing under the Americans with Disabilities Act: Empirical Answers, and Some Questions." *Temple Political & Civil Rights Law Review* 9(2): 237–52.

Carpenter, Christine. 1994. "The Experience of Spinal Cord Injury: The Individual's Perspective—Implications for Rehabilitation Practice." *Physical Therapy* 74(7): 614–27.

Chamallas, Martha, and Jennifer B. Wriggins. 2010. *The Measure of Injury: Race, Gender, and Tort Law*. New York: New York University Press.

Chang, Jung. 2003. *Wild Swans: Three Daughters of China*. New York: Touchstone.

Chapman, C. Richard. 1995. "The Affective Dimension of Pain: A Model." In *Pain and the Brain: From Nociception to Cognition*, edited by Burkhart Bromm and John E. Desmedt, 283–301. New York: Raven Press.

Coates, Dan, and Steven Penrod. 1980–81. "Social Psychology and the Emergence of Disputes." *Law & Society Review* 15(3/4): 655–80.

Cohen, H. Harvey. 2000. "A Field Study of Stair Descent." *Ergonomics in Design: The Quarterly of Human Factors Applications* 8: 11–12.

Cohen, Joseph. 2009. "Stairway Falls: An Ergonomics Analysis of 80 Cases." *Professional Safety: Journal of the American Society of Safety Engineers* 27: 32.

Cohen, Thomas H. 2009. "Tort Bench and Jury Trials in State Courts, 2005." *Bureau of Justice Statistics Bulletin* 1–15. Washington, DC: U.S. Department of Justice, Office of Justice Programs.

Cohen, Thomas H., and Kyle Harbacek. 2011. "Punitive Damage Awards in State Courts, 2005." *Bureau of Justice Statistics Special Reports* 1–11. Washington, DC: U.S. Department of Justice, Office of Justice Programs.

Cook, Douglas H. 2004. "A Faith-Based Perspective on Tort Causation." *St. Thomas Law Review* 16: 455–72.

Cowell, Alan. 2011. "Garret FitzGerald, Ex-Irish Premier, Dies at 85." *New York Times*, May 19. Accessed November 4, 2015. http://www.nytimes.com/2011/05/20/world/europe/20fitzgerald.html?_r=0.

Cranz, Galen. 1998. *The Chair: Rethinking Culture, Body, and Design*. New York: W. W. Norton.

Crockett, David J., Kenneth M. Prkachin, and Kenneth D. Craig. 1977–78. "Factors of the Language of Pain in Patient and Volunteer Groups." *Pain* 4: 175–82.

Csordas, Thomas J. 1994. "Introduction: The Body as Representation and Being-in-the-World." In *Embodiment and Experience: The Existential Ground of Culture and Self*, edited by Thomas J. Csordas, 1–24. New York: Cambridge University Press.

———. 2011. "Embodiment: Agency, Sexual Difference, and Illness." In *A Companion to the Anthropology of the Body and Embodiment*, edited by Frances E. Mascia-Lees, 137–56. Chichester, UK: Wiley-Blackwell.

Damasio, Antonio. 2012. *Self Comes to Mind: Constructing the Conscious Brain*. New York: Vintage Books.

Daniels, Stephen, and Joanne Martin. 2000. " 'The Impact That It Has Had Is between People's Ears': Tort Reform, Mass Culture, and Plaintiffs' Lawyers." *DePaul Law Review* 50(2): 453–96.

Daudet, Alphonse. 2002 [1930]. *In the Land of Pain*. Edited and translated by Julian Barnes. New York: Alfred A. Knopf.

Davis, Dena S. 2001. "Male and Female Genital Alteration: A Collision Course with the Law?" *Health Matrix: Journal of Law-Medicine* 11(2): 487–570.

Davis, Joshua Ian, and Arthur B. Markman. 2012. "Embodied Cognition as a Practical Paradigm: Introduction to the Topic, The Future of Embodied Cognition." *Topics in Cognitive Science* 4: 685–91.

de Vignemont, Frederique. 2011. "Embodiment, Ownership and Disownership." *Consciousness & Cognition* 20(1): 82–93.

Devito, Scott, and Andrew W. Jurs. 2014. " 'Doubling-Down' for Defendants: The Pernicious Effects of Tort Reform." *Penn State Law Review* 118(3): 543–99.

Doyle, Arthur Conan. 1930. *The Complete Sherlock Holmes*. New York: Double Day.

Dunbar, Frederick C., and Faten Sabry. 2007. "The Propensity to Sue: Why Do People Seek Legal Actions?" *Business Economics* 42(2): 31–42.

Dvorak, August. 1943. "There Is a Better Typewriter Keyboard." *National Business Education Quarterly* 12(2): 51–66.

Echterhoff, Gerald E., Tory Higgins, and John M. Levine. 2009. "Shared Reality: Experiencing Commonality with Others' Inner States about the World." *Perspectives on Psychological Science* 4(5): 496–521.

Eisenberg, Theodore. 2013. "The Empirical Effects of Tort Reform." In *Research Handbook on the Economics of Torts*, edited by Jennifer Arlen, 513–50. Cheltenham, UK: Edward Elgar Publishing.

Eliot, T. S. 1952. *The Complete Poems and Plays*. New York: Harcourt, Brace and Company.

Engel, David M. 1983. "Cases, Conflict, and Accommodation: Patterns of Legal Interaction in an American Community." *Law and Social Inquiry [American Bar Foundation Research Journal]* 8(4): 803–74.

———. 1984. "The Oven Bird's Song: Insiders, Outsiders, and Personal Injuries in an American Community." *Law & Society Review* 18(4): 551–82.

Engel, David M., and Jaruwan S. Engel. 2010. *Tort, Custom, and Karma: Globalization and Legal Consciousness in Thailand*. Stanford, CA: Stanford University Press.

Engel, David M., and Frank W. Munger. 2003. *Rights of Inclusion: Law and Identity in the Life Stories of Americans with Disabilities*. Chicago: University of Chicago Press.

Engstrom, Nora Freeman. 2011. "Sunlight and Settlement Mills." *New York University Law Review* 86(4): 805–86.

Erichson, Howard M. 2005. "A Typology of Aggregate Settlements." *Notre Dame Law Review* 80: 1769–820.

Fateh-Moghadam, Bijan. 2012. "Criminalizing Male Circumcision? Case Note: Landericht Cologne, Judgment of 7 May 2012—No. 151 Ns 169/11." *German Law Journal* 13(9): 1131–45.

Fein, Ronald A., and Janet Cooper Alexander. 2003. "Appendix: The History and Structure of the September 11th Victim Compensation Fund." *DePaul Law Review* 53(2): 692–718.

Felstiner, William L. F. 1974. "Influences of Social Organization on Dispute Processing." *Law & Society Review* 9(1): 63–94.

Felstiner, William L. F., Richard L. Abel, and Austin Sarat. 1980–81. "The Emergence and Transformation of Disputes: Naming, Blaming, Claiming . . ." *Law & Society Review* 15(3–4): 631–54.

Fineman, Martha Albertson. 2008. "The Vulnerable Subject: Anchoring Equality in the Human Condition." *Yale Journal of Law & Feminism* 20(1): 1–23.

Finley, Lucinda M. 2004. "The Hidden Victims of Tort Reform: Women, Children, and the Elderly." *Emory Law Journal* 53(3): 1263–314.

FitzGerald, Jeffrey. 1983. "Grievances, Disputes and Outcomes: A Comparison of Australia and the United States." *Law in Context* 1: 15–45.

Fitzpatrick, Brian T. 2015. "The End of Class Actions?" *Arizona Law Review* 57(1): 161–99.

Fox, Marie, and Michael Thomson. 2009. "Foreskin Is a Feminist Issue." *Australian Feminist Studies* 24(60): 195–210.

Franklin, Gary M., and Lorene Nelson. 2003. "Environmental Risk Factors in

Multiple Sclerosis: Causes, Triggers, and Patient Autonomy." *Neurology* 61: 1032–34.

Free, Mary Moore. 2002. "Cross Cultural Conceptions of Pain and Pain Control." *Baylor University Medical Center Proceedings* 15(2): 143–45.

Friedman, Lawrence M. 1985. *Total Justice.* New York: Russell Sage Foundation.

———. 1990. *The Republic of Choice: Law, Authority, and Culture.* Cambridge, MA: Harvard University Press.

Galanter, Marc. 1974. "Why the 'Haves' Come Out Ahead: Speculations on the Limits of Legal Change." *Law & Society Review* 9(1): 95–160.

———. 1983. "Reading the Landscape of Disputes: What We Know and Don't Know (and Think We Know) about Our Allegedly Contentious and Litigious Society." *UCLA Law Review* 31(1): 4–72.

———. 1996. "Real World Torts: An Antidote to Anecdote." *Maryland Law Review* 55(4): 1093–160.

Geertz, Clifford. 1973. *The Interpretation of Cultures.* New York: Basic Books.

———. 1983. *Local Knowledge: Further Essays in Interpretive Anthropology.* New York: Basic Books.

Genn, Hazel. 1999. *Paths to Justice: What People Do and Think about Going to Law.* Portland, OR: Hart Publishing.

Genn, Hazel, and Alan Paterson. 2001. *Paths to Justice Scotland: What People in Scotland Do and Think about Going to Law.* Portland, OR: Hart Publishing.

Gergen, Kenneth J. 1994. *Toward Transformation in Social Knowledge,* 2nd ed. Thousand Oaks, CA: Sage Publications.

Glenberg, Arthur M. 2010. "Embodiment as a Unifying Perspective for Psychology." *Wiley Interdisciplinary Reviews: Cognitive Science* 1: 586–96.

Goffman, Erving. 1963. *Stigma: Notes on the Management of Spoiled Identity.* Englewood Cliffs, NJ: Prentice-Hall.

Greenberg, Lynne. 2009. *The Body Broken.* New York: Random House.

Greenhouse, Carol J., Barbara Yngvesson, and David M. Engel. 1994. *Law and Community in Three American Towns.* Ithaca, NY: Cornell University Press.

Haidt, Jonathan. 2012. *The Righteous Mind: Why Good People Are Divided by Politics and Religion.* New York: Pantheon Books.

Haltom, William, and Michael McCann. 2004. *Distorting the Law: Politics, Media, and the Litigation Crisis.* Chicago: University of Chicago Press.

Hardin, Curtis, and Terri Conley. 2001. "A Relational Approach to Cognition: Shared Experience and Relationship Affirmation in Social Cognition." In *Cognitive Social Psychology: The Princeton Symposium on the Legacy and Future of Social Cognition,* edited by Gordon B. Moskowitz, 3–17. Mahwah, NJ: Lawrence Erlbaum Associates.

Hebert, Camille. 2007. "Why Don't 'Reasonable Women' Complain about Sexual Harassment?" *Indiana Law Journal* 82(3): 711–43.

Henderson, Jr., James A., and Theodore Eisenberg. 1990. "The Quiet Revolution in Products Liability: An Empirical Study of Legal Change." *UCLA Law Review* 37(3): 479–553.

Hensler, Deborah R., M. Susan Marquis, Allan F. Abrahamse, Sandra H. Berry, Patricia A. Ebener, Elizabeth G. Lewis, E. Allan Lind, Robert J. MacCoun, Willard G. Manning, Jeannette A. Rogowski, and Mary E. Vaiana. 1991. *Compensation for Accidental Injuries in the United States*. Santa Monica, CA: RAND.

Heshusius, Lous. 2009. *Inside Chronic Pain: An Intimate and Critical Account*. Ithaca, NY: ILR Press.

Hickson, Gerald B., Ellen Wright Clayton, Jenny B. Githens, and Frank A. Sloan. 1992. "Factors That Prompted Families to File Medical Malpractice Claims Following Perinatal Injuries." *Journal of the American Medical Association* 267(10): 1359–63.

Hofvander, Yngve. 2002. "New Law on Male Circumcision in Sweden (Correspondence)." *Lancet* 359: 630.

Hovenkamp, Herbert. 1982. "Pragmatic Realism and Proximate Cause in America." *Journal of Legal History* 3(1): 3–30.

Howe, P. David. 2001. "An Ethnography of Pain and Injury in Professional Rugby Union." *International Review for the Sociology of Sport* 36: 289–303.

Hume, David. 1999. *An Enquiry Concerning Human Understanding*. Edited by Tom L. Beauchamp. New York: Oxford University Press.

Hurwitz, David, Anuj Pradhan, Donald L. Fisher, Michael A. Knodler, Jeffrey W. Muttart, Rajiv Menon, and Uwe Meissner. 2010. "Backing Collisions: A Study of Drivers' Eye and Backing Behaviour Using Combined Rear-View Camera and Sensor Systems." *Injury Prevention* 16(2): 79–84.

Issacharoff, Samuel, and John Fabian Witt. 2004. "The Inevitability of Aggregate Settlement: An Institutional Account of American Tort Law." *Vanderbilt Law Review* 57(5): 1571–636.

Jackson, Jean E. 1994. "Chronic Pain and the Tension between the Body as Subject and Object." In *Embodiment and Experience: The Existential Ground of Culture and Self*, edited by Thomas J. Csordas, 201–28. Cambridge: Cambridge University Press.

———. 2011. "Pain and Bodies." In *A Companion to the Anthropology of the Body and Embodiment*, edited by Frances E. Mascia-Lees, 370–87. Chichester, UK: Wiley-Blackwell.

Jackson, Patricia L., and H. Harvey Cohen. 1995. "An In-Depth Investigation of 40-Stairway Accidents and the Stair Safety Literature." *Journal of Safety Research* 26(3): 151–59.

Jain, Sarah S. Lochlann. 2006. *Injury: The Politics of Product Design and Safety Law in the United States*. Princeton, NJ: Princeton University Press.

Johansson, Eva E., Katarina Hamberg, Göran Westman, and Gerd Lindgren. 1999. "The Meanings of Pain: An Exploration of Women's Descriptions of Symptoms." *Social Science & Medicine* 48(12): 1791–802.

Johnson, Mark. 2007. *The Meaning of the Body: Aesthetics of Human Understanding*. Chicago: University of Chicago Press.

Jost, John T., Alison Ledgerwood, and Curtis D. Hardin. 2008. "Shared Reality, System Justification, and the Relational Basis of Ideological Beliefs." *Social and Personality Psychology Compass* 2(1): 171–86.

Kahneman, Daniel. 2011. *Thinking, Fast and Slow*. New York: Farrar, Straus and Giroux.

Kelman, Mark. 2011. *The Heuristics Debate*. New York: Oxford University Press.

Kepe, Thembela. 2010. "'Secrets' That Kill: Crisis, Custodianship and Responsibility in Ritual Male Circumcision in the Eastern Cape Province, South Africa." *Social Science & Medicine* 70(5): 729–35.

Kleinman, Arthur. 1992. "Pain and Resistance: The Delegitimation and Relegitimation of Local Worlds." In *Pain as Human Experience: An Anthropological Perspective*, edited by Mary-Jo DelVecchio Good, Paul E. Brodwin, Byron J. Good, and Arthur Kleinman, 169–97. Los Angeles: University of California Press.

Kritzer, Herbert M. 2004. *Risks, Reputations, and Rewards: Contingency Fee Legal Practice in the United States*. Stanford, CA: Stanford University Press.

Kritzer, Herbert M., W. A. Bogart, and Neil Vidmar. 1991. "The Aftermath of Injury: Cultural Factors in Compensation Seeking in Canada and the United States." *Law & Society Review* 25(3): 499–543.

Kumar, Adarsh, Mathew Varghese, and Dinesh Mohan. 2000. "Equipment-Related Injuries in Agriculture: An International Perspective." *Injury Control & Safety Promotion* 7(3): 175–86.

Lakoff, George, and Mark Johnson. 1999. *Philosophy in the Flesh: The Embodied Mind and Its Challenge to Western Thought*. New York: Basic Books.

Landro, Laura. 2007. "Doctors Learn to Say 'I'm Sorry': Patients' Stories of Hospital Errors Serve to Teach Staff." *Wall Street Journal*, January 24. Accessed August 9, 2015. http://online.wsj.com/articles /SB116960074741385710.

Lave, Charles A., and James G. March. 1993. *An Introduction to Models in the Social Sciences*. Lanham, MD: University Press of America.

Levine, James. 2014. "Killer Chairs: How Desk Jobs Ruin Your Health." *Scientific American* 311: 34–35.

Levy, Howard S. 1966. *Chinese Footbinding: The History of a Curious Erotic Custom.* New York: Walton Rawls.

Lienert, Anita. 2013. "Feds, Safety Advocates Fight over Rearview Camera." *Edmunds*, September 25. Accessed August 9, 2015. http://www.edmunds .com/car-news/feds-safety-advocates-fight-over-rear-view-camera -recommendation.html.

Lovallo, Dan, and Daniel Kahneman. 2003. "Delusions of Success: How Optimism Undermines Executives' Decisions." *Harvard Business Review* 81(7): 56–63.

Lucas, Jennifer L. 2003. "Drivers' Psychological and Physical Reactions after Motor Vehicle Accidents." *Transportation Research Part F* 6(2): 135–45.

Mackie, Gerry. 1996. "Ending Footbinding and Infibulation: A Convention Account." *American Sociological Review* 61(6): 999–1017.

MacLennan, Carol A. 1988. "From Accident to Crash: The Auto Industry and the Politics of Injury." *Medical Anthropology Quarterly* 2(3): 239–45.

Malone, Wex S. 1956. "Ruminations on Cause-in-Fact." *Stanford Law Review* 9(1): 60–99.

Manning, Bayless. 1977. "Hyperlexis: Our National Disease." *Northwestern University Law Review* 71(6): 767–82.

Mather, Lynn. 2009. "Lawyers and Solicitors Separated by a Common Legal System: Anti-Tobacco Litigation in the United States and Britain." In *Fault Lines: Tort Law as Cultural Practice*, edited by David M. Engel and Michael McCann, 192–210. Stanford, CA: Stanford University Press.

McGarity, Thomas O. 2013. *Freedom to Harm: The Lasting Legacy of the Laissez Faire Revival.* New Haven, CT: Yale University Press.

Mearns, Hughes. n.d. "Antigonish [I met a man who wasn't there]." Accessed August 20, 2015. http://www.poets.org/poetsorg/poem/antigonish-i-met -man-who-wasnt-there.

Mencken, H. L. 1919. *Prejudices: First Series.* New York: Alfred A. Knopf.

Merleau-Ponty, Maurice. 1958. *Phenomenology of Perception.* Translated by Colin Smith. New York: Routledge and Kegan Paul.

Michelson, Ethan. 2007. "Climbing the Dispute Pagoda: Grievances and Appeals to the Official Justice System in Rural China." *American Sociological Review* 72(3): 459–85.

Miller, Arthur R. 2014. "The Preservation and Rejuvenation of Aggregate Litigation: A Systemic Imperative." *Emory Law Journal* 64(2): 293–327.

Miller, Richard E., and Austin Sarat. 1980–81. "Grievances, Claims, and Disputes: Assessing the Adversary Culture." *Law & Society Review* 15(3/4): 525–66.

Murayama, Masayuki. 2007. "Experiences of Problems and Disputing Behaviour in Japan." *Meiji Law Journal* 14: 1–59.

Nadler, Janice. 2012. "Blaming as a Social Process: The Influence of Character and Moral Emotion on Blame." *Law and Contemporary Problems* 75(2): 1–31.

National Multiple Sclerosis Society. N.d. "Clusters." Accessed September 4, 2015. www.nationalmssociety.org/What-is-MS/What-Causes-MS/Clusters.

National Safety Council. 2014. *Injury Facts, 2014 Edition*. Itasca, IL: National Safety Council.

Nedelsky, Jennifer. 2011. *Law's Relations: A Relational Theory of Self, Autonomy, and Law*. New York: Oxford University Press.

Nockleby, John T., and Shannon Curreri. 2005. "100 Years of Conflict: The Past and Future of Tort Retrenchment." *Loyola of Los Angeles Law Review* 38(3/2): 1021–91.

Noyes, Jan. 1983. "The QWERTY Keyboard: A Review." *International Journal of Man-Machine Studies* 18(3): 265–81.

Office of Regulatory Analysis and Evaluation, National Center for Statistics and Analysis. 2014 . "Backover Crash Avoidance Technologies." FMVSS No. 111, Final Regulatory Impact Analysis, National Highway Traffic Safety Administration, U.S. Department of Transportation.

Pace, Nicholas M., Daniela Golinelli, and Laura Zakaras. 2004. "Capping Non-Economic Awards in Medical Malpractice Trials: California Jury Verdicts under MICRA." Santa Monica: RAND.

Pauls, J. L. 1991. "Safety Standards, Requirements, and Litigation in Relation to Building Use and Safety, Especially Safety from Falls Involving Stairs." *Safety Science* 14: 125–54.

Pennington, Donald C., Kate Gillen, and Pam Hill. 1999. *Social Psychology*. New York: Oxford University Press.

Posner, Richard. 1972. "A Theory of Negligence." *Journal of Legal Studies* 1: 29–96.

Rabin, Robert L. 2012. "The John G. Fleming Lecture: A Brief History of Accident Law—Tort and the Administrative State." *Tort Law Review* 20: 11–18.

Rabin, Roni Caryn. 2010. "Steep Drop Seen in Circumcisions in U.S." *New York Times*, August 16. http://www.nytimes.com/2010/08/17/health/research/17circ.html?_r=0. Accessed August 12, 2015.

Radnofsky, Louise. 2007. "Mission: Car Safety." *Newsday*, February 28. Accessed August 12, 2015. http://www.newsday.com/news/mission-car-safety-1.666993.

Robbennolt, Jennifer K. 2003. "Apologies and Legal Settlement: An Empirical Examination." *Michigan Law Review* 102(3): 460–516.

Rosenwald, George C. 1992. "Conclusion: Reflections on Narrative Self-Understanding." In *Storied Lives: The Cultural Politics of Self-Understanding*, edited by George C. Rosenwald and Richard L. Ochberg, 265–89. New Haven, CT: Yale University Press.

Ross, H. Laurence. 1980. *Settled Out of Court: The Social Process of Insurance Claims Adjustment*, 2nd ed. Hawthorne, NY, Aldine.

Saks, Michael J. 1992. "Do We Really Know Anything about the Behavior of the Tort Litigation System—and Why Not?" *University of Pennsylvania Law Review* 140(4): 1147–292.

Samuelson, William, and Richard Zeckhauser. 1988. "Status Quo Bias in Decision Making." *Journal of Risk and Uncertainty* 1: 7–59.

Scarry, Elaine. 1985. *The Body in Pain: The Making and Unmaking of the World*. New York: Oxford University Press.

Schank, Roger C., and Robert P. Abelson. 1977. *Scripts, Plans, Goals and Understanding: An Inquiry into Human Knowledge Structures*. Hillsdale, MI: Lawrence Erlbaum Associates.

Schuck, Peter H. 2008. "Tort Reform, Kiwi-Style." *Yale Law and Policy Review* 27(1): 187–203.

Schulz, Richard, and Susan Decker. 1985. "Long-Term Adjustment to Physical Disability: The Role of Social Support, Perceived Control and Self-Blame." *Journal of Personality and Social Psychology* 48(5): 1162–72.

Schwartz, Gary. 1992. "The Beginning and the Possible End of the Rise of Modern American Tort Law." *Georgia Law Review* 26(3): 601–702.

Silverman, Eric K. 2004. "Anthropology and Circumcision." *Annual Review of Anthropology* 33(1): 419–45.

Sloan, Frank A., and Chee Ruey Hsieh. 1995. "Injury, Liability, and the Decision to File a Medical Malpractice Claim." *Law & Society Review* 29(3): 413–35.

Stewart, Larry S., Daniel L. Cohen, and Karen L. Marangi. 2002. "The September 11th Victim Compensation Fund: Past or Prologue?" *Connecticut Insurance Law Journal* 9: 153–78.

Stinchcombe, Arthur L. 1968. *Constructing Social Theories*. New York: Harcourt, Brace and World.

Thaler, Richard H., and Cass R. Sunstein. 2008. *Nudge: Improving Decisions about Health, Wealth, and Happiness*. New Haven, CT: Yale University Press.

Tunstrøm, Kolbjørn, Yael Katz, Christos C. Ioannou, Cristián Huepe, Matthew J. Lutz, and Iain D. Couzin. 2013. "Collective States, Multistability and Transitional Behavior in Schooling Fish." *PLoS Computational Biology* 9(2): 1–11.

Voltaire. 1919. "To Frederick William, Prince of Prussia." In *Voltaire in His Letters: Being a Selection from His Correspondence*, translated and edited by S. G. Tallentyre, 231–33. New York: G. P. Putnam's Sons.

Waldeck, Sarah E. 2003. "Using Male Circumcision to Understand Social Norms as Multipliers." *University of Cincinnati Law Review* 72(2): 455–526.

Wallace, David Foster. 2009. *This Is Water: Some Thoughts Delivered on a Significant Occasion, about Living a Compassionate Life*. New York: Little, Brown and Company.

Ward, Ashley J. W., David J. T. Sumpter, Iain D. Couzin, Paul J. B. Hart, and Jens Krause. 2008. "Quorum Decision-Making Facilitates Information Transfer in Fish Shoals." *Proceedings of the National Academy of Sciences* 105(19): 6948–53.

Watson, S. J. 2011. *Before I Go to Sleep*. New York: HarperCollins.

Webster's Unabridged Dictionary of the English Language. 2001. New York: Random House.

Weila, Michael J. 2012. "The Friendly Separation of Church and State and Bans on Male Circumcision." *Connecticut Law Review* 45(2): 695–742.

Wenner, David. 2003. "Juror Bias." In *Litigating Tort Cases, Volume 3*, edited by Roxanne Barton Conlin and Gregory S. Cusimano, chapter 35. Washington, DC: AAJ Press.

Wilde, Mary H. 2003. "Embodied Knowledge in Chronic Illness and Injury." *Nursing Inquiry* 10(3): 170–76.

Williams, Lawrence E., and John A. Bargh. 2008. "Experiencing Physical Warmth Promotes Interpersonal Warmth." *Science* 322(5901): 606–7.

Wright, Beatrice Ann Posner. 1983. *Physical Disability: A Psychosocial Approach*, 2nd ed. New York: Harper and Row.

Zollers, Frances E., Sandra N. Hurd, and Peter Shears. 2000. "Looking Backward, Looking Forward: Reflections on Twenty Years of Product Liability Reform." *Syracuse Law Review* 50(3): 1019–53.

STATUTES, REGULATIONS, AND CASES

Cipollone v. Liggett Group, Inc., 112 S.Ct. 2608 (1992).

Department of Transportation, National Highway Traffic Safety Administration, 49 CFR Part 571, Docket No. NHTSA-2010-0162, RIN 2127-AK43.

Dreisonstok v. Volkswagenwerk, 489 F.2d 1066 (4th Cir. 1974).

Fishbeck v. State of North Dakota, 115 F.3d 580 (8th Cir. 1997).

Flatt ex rel. Flatt v. Kantak, 687 N.W.2d 208 (N.D. 2004).

Grimshaw v. Ford Motor Company, 119 Cal. App. 3d 757 (Cal. Ct. App. 1981).

In re Marriage of Boldt, 176 P.3d 388 (Or. 2008).

Medical Injury Compensation Reform Act (MICRA). 1975 Cal. Stat. 3494-4007, codified at Cal. Civ. Code § 3333.2 (1997).

Montesinos v. Daly, No. 105868/2007, 2009 WL 994790 (N.Y. Sup. Ct. April 2, 2009).

New York Central Railroad v. Grimstad, 264 F. 334 (2d Cir. 1920).

Zinnel v. U.S. Shipping Board Emergency Fleet Corporation, 10 F.2d 47 (2d Cir. 1925).

INDEX

Page numbers in italic refer to figures and tables.